Mountaineering in Prayer

Freda Flude

New Wine Press

New Wine Press
P.O. Box 17
Chichester
England

First published by New Wine Press in 1985

Unless otherwise stated biblical references are taken from the Authorised Version.

ISBN 0 947852 09 3

CONTENTS

Preface

There are so many facets to prayer and so much to be discovered in our walk with the Lord; it is like seeking treasure — treasure for the finding!

Praying is not a drudgery, as I used to think, neither is it something to be fitted into the day or just a discipline of the Christian life. Prayer is a way of life; it has within its sphere scope to suit every stage of growth.

We need to keep a sense of adventure; the inquisitive exploration of an infant, the treasure collecting of a child, as well as the more disciplined pursuit of a craft or skill made by an adult.

I am sure the Holy Spirit is mindful of our own personalities, and leads us in avenues of prayer which are just right for our growth and which give us delight as persons. He also gives us burdens to carry which He knows are within our range.

One thing I have learned is that I do not have to try to have someone else's experience. I do not have to fit into a prayer mould; I just have to develop. A young infant discovering that a ball can roll and move along the floor may one day become a skilled tennis player or footballer. So it is with prayer, and my encouragement for those who love the Lord is to be childlike enough to delight in the oneness to be found with the Lord concerning even what could be termed simple and unimportant matters, and to become mature enough to move skilfully and adeptly, as one trained and disciplined in an acquired art.

1

An Aspiring Beginner

To define prayer, I would have to use many expressions and words, for prayer is having communion with the Lord — having a conversation with Him — getting to know Him — experiencing intimate fellowship — enjoying His presence — sharing joys and sorrows with Him — seeking His advice and understanding — receiving instruction and guidance — being directed to see as He sees — comprehending the authority of His name — discovering the greatness of God and worshipping Him.

The terms and expressions which could be used in place of the word 'prayer' are almost endless; and yet so often we hold on to one concept of prayer, which often has been gained in our younger years by hearing other people pray or attending prayer meetings.

My earliest remembrance of prayer is repeating a rhymed verse before going to sleep. Later, as a nine-year-old, I had to kneel quietly while members of my family and guests prayed long prayers concerning the evening service after the tea-time meal on Sundays. I had just wanted them to say 'Amen' so that the prayers would be ended quickly!

On becoming a Christian at twenty-nine years old, my concept of prayer meetings did not change, for there seemed to be the same pattern that I had listened to as a child taking place in prayer meetings. Some of the prayers were muttered so that I could not hear them, and others seemed to repeat a similar prayer each week — and only very rarely were answers discussed or shared. Problems which had been named in prayer so often remained problems.

The Lord, in His own loving way, began to show me that I could talk to Him about little things as well as my anxieties and fears and the bigger problems which I encountered. I began to discover that He was interested in every detail of my life and that He delights to have my conversation and fellowship.

In my earlier days as a Christian, I was sometimes asked to speak at meetings for children and young people. I had bought a book which gave ideas for talks, and would search diligently through that book to get my guidance.

On one occasion I chose a talk which took various kinds of hats to bring out certain aspects of the gospel message. I decided that it would be much more interesting if I could have the hats to show to the children, and went into action to either collect or make what was needed.

It was not too difficult to make a Chinese coolie hat and a chef's hat, and I was able to borrow an Army hat from the young man next door who was in the Army Cadets. Then I had to do something about the more difficult types of hat that I required.

I decided to go to the police station and ask if I could borrow one of their helmets. There were about half a dozen policemen standing around, and I had to get past my embarrassment at their laughter, but when one of them asked why I wanted to borrow one of their helmets, I not only told them the reason for my request but the aspect of the gospel that this hat would bring out to the young people.

I was readily given a helmet after signing a paper promising to return it. It was a strange feeling to walk out of the police station with a policeman's helmet tucked under my arm!

I then made my way to the fire station to borrow a fireman's helmet, and was shown into the office of the chief fire officer and his assistant. Once again I made my request known, and again was asked my reason for wanting to borrow a helmet. I took this opportunity also to share both the reason and the aspect of the gospel shown by the fireman's helmet. My request was granted and I emerged with my second triumph!

I needed a coal miner's helmet for my talk, and pondered where I would get such a hat. On sharing with a friend, she remembered a certain coal merchant in town who for years had displayed a coal miner's helmet in the shop window. I immediately went along and enquired if I could borrow the helmet he had on display. After a slight hesitation I was granted the use of it on the promise to return it within a few days.

Gradually my hats were accumulated, but the all-important one evaded me. This was a naval captain's hat, which would bring out the climax of my talk that Jesus is the Captain of our salvation. I asked many people, including a lady in our church who had often dealt with costumes for a drama group. I also went to a local shop where theatrical costumes could be hired, but all without success.

The day of my talk arrived and I felt so disappointed that I had not been able to find the most important hat. I had cycled into the town to do a little shopping, and as I was pushing my bicycle up a hill on my homeward journey I was talking to the Lord. I told Him that I was disappointed concerning the naval captain's hat and that it seemed that all my efforts to get the other hats were wasted — because without the one that really portrayed Him, I felt the whole message would fall flat.

The hill which I was climbing with my head cast down was completely empty of traffic and there were no people. I said, "Well, Lord, I suppose I can use the other hats now I have gone to all the trouble to collect them, but I did want the most important one. I have tried every possible avenue and only You know if there is a hat available in the town like the one I require."

Almost immediately a door opened on the other side of the road and a naval man emerged wearing a peaked cap just like the one I wanted! I did not think it was a captain's hat, but I knew that it was near enough for the children. I stopped in amazement and watched that man as he started to walk down the hill. He glanced over in my direction, no doubt wondering why I was staring at him.

I did not know what to do. I said, "Lord, there goes my hat!"

My heart pounded madly and I watched as the man turned the corner and disappeared out of sight. I thought, "It must be the Lord to bring that man out of the house at this time, but he is wearing the hat and how can I get ?"

I decided that I must not let the opportunity pass by, and, not knowing what I was going to say, I turned my bicycle round, pedalled after that man and caught up with him in the next road. I pulled up alongside him, and said rather breathlessly, "Excuse me, but do you know where I can get a hat like the one you are wearing?"

I shall never forget the expression on the man's face, but I hastily added my reason for wanting a naval peaked hat. He was silent for a moment and then said, "When are you wanting this hat, and for how long will you want it?"

After I had told him he replied, "You can borrow this one if you can collect it on your way to the meeting and promise to return it on your way home."

My heart leapt with joy. Not only had God heard me, but He had answered my prayer. What a miracle that the man should walk out of the house just as I was walking up that hilly road talking to the Lord about the hat. Not only did I have my illustrated talk to give to the children, but I could relate the miracle of God's working power to provide what was needed for my talk.

Only now, as I reflect back, do I realise that the Holy Spirit was working upon that man — first to bring him out of the house at that precise moment, and also to cause him to be willing to let me have the use of his hat.

2

Equipment for Climbing

When I received the Lord Jesus as my Saviour, I told the Lord that I wanted my life to be fully His, and that I wanted to do His will and to please Him.

This commitment, which I have renewed or expressed many many times since that first occasion, has helped me to value my walk with the Lord. Not only has Jesus redeemed me and set me free from the law of sin and death, but I have chosen with the free will that He gave to me to be His bondslave. I tried in every way I possibly could to fulfil that commitment. I was always wanting to do things for the Lord, and in the midst of my activity I had no idea how He was working in me — using every endeavour that I made to bring me into the reality of my commitment, to show me that a walk of faith was needed to please Him, and to bring me to a place where I did not work for Him but *with* Him.

After ten years of being a Christian, I was dismayed to realise how discontented I had become. I was putting everything that I possibly could into the Sunday School work that He had given to me, but I could not understand the dissatisfaction that continued to plague me.

This dissatisfaction drove me to a little evangelical church on Sunday evenings, thinking I would find satisfaction in a different place of worship. It also drove me to a Christian bookshop, where I was forever trying to find another book which would give me new insight.

I often told the Lord I was sorry for feeling the way I did, for I was convinced that He should completely satisfy me, and there I was in the midst of feelings and an experience I could not understand, and from which I could not get free even after telling the Lord that I was sorry about it.

I had no way of knowing at that time that I was hungering for more of the Lord, that the hunger within me was a divine one and would eventually lead me into a new depth of experience with Him.

A peace came to me after I had poured out my heart in prayer one evening. I had told the Lord that I wished I had been born when His first disciples were born; I would love to have lived then, because not only were souls saved but the sick were healed and the dead were raised. I repeated my statement to Him, declaring that if I could have had my choice I would have chosen to be one of His first disciples.

The Lord found a way to answer my cry to Him. I had not read any books concerning the baptism in the Holy Spirit; if they were in existence, I had not found them. Neither had I met anyone who talked about this experience; if any had received it, they kept quiet about it.

I had always assumed that what had happened on the day of Pentecost, when the disciples were gathered in the upper room, was an experience just for them, and how I envied them. The Lord had told the disciples that they were not to leave Jerusalem but were to wait for the promise of the Father by being baptised with the Holy Spirit (Acts 1:4 – 5). He told them that they would receive power after the Holy Spirit had come upon them.

In some ways I still envy them their experience, for they heard a sound from heaven as of a rushing mighty wind, and saw cloven tongues like as of fire which sat upon each of them, and they were all filled with the Holy Spirit and **all** began to speak with other tongues. The people who heard them recognised the languages which they were speaking and which they had not learnt.

My experience of receiving the promise of the Father by being baptised with the Holy Spirit was exactly opposite to that of those early disciples. I did not hear anything, I did not see anything, and I did not speak in a new language. I just wept for joy that there was something new to receive from the Lord.

I had ministry similar to the Samaritans, for we read in Acts chapter eight that Philip had been preaching to them and they had believed God when they heard the preaching and saw miracles. Even Simon the sorcerer believed and was baptised in water. When the apostles who were in Jerusalem heard that Samaria had received the word of God, they sent Peter and John, who laid hands upon those Samaritans that they might receive the Holy Spirit. The baptism of the Holy Spirit was a separate experience to their believing and being baptised in water. There must have been some evidence that they had received because Simon offered money to receive also. Could this have been that they were speaking in tongues?

Two days after I had had the laying on of hands to receive the baptism in the Holy Spirit, I was asked by the minister who had prayed for me if I had spoken in tongues. When I replied 'No', he said he would pray for me again that I might have that gift.

He gave me some instructions, telling me that I needed to take a step of faith, for in order for the Holy Spirit within me to give me the gift of speaking in tongues or a new language, I had to give Him the vehicle or the avenue through which He could work — my mouth, my tongue and my vocal chords. If I sat with my mouth shut, there would be no speaking in tongues. If I took the step of faith by producing a sound and moving my mouth, I would receive my gift. I could produce the avenue but not the language. The Holy Spirit could produce the language when given the avenue.

I had a dreadful battle with my self-consciousness, but I knew that I must obey the instruction given to me; and so, after prayer, I began as instructed. After only two or three halting syllables I stopped, as I felt stupid, like a baby trying to talk and not knowing how.

The minister said with much confidence, "There you are. What is wrong with that?"

I replied, "Is ***that*** it?"

"Of course it is," he answered, "and if you continue you will get a flow." He left me with those words.

On my own, I said to the Lord, "I know that You have called that man to the ministry. I have seen the evidence of Your calling and the signs that have followed his preaching, for many sick have been healed as well as many souls saved." I continued, "He says those two or three syllables are my new language and I am going to believe it, but I am not satisfied. I would like to have a flow, but I will use the little until You give me more."

Looking back, I realise that this set me free from struggling or analysing, and I can honestly say that as the days continued, and I used my gift, the flow increased.

Just as the experience of salvation is so varied amongst Christians, so also is the experience of the baptism in the Holy Spirit. It is interesting to read how Paul met believers in Ephesus and asked them if they had received the Holy Spirit since they believed, and they answered, **"We have not even heard that there is a Holy Spirit" (Acts 19 NIV).** They had been baptised **"unto John's baptism",** but Paul gave them instruction. We read that they were than **"baptised into the name of the Lord Jesus. When Paul placed his hands on them, the Holy Spirit came on them, and they spoke in tongues and prophesied."** There were a number of years between this incident and the day of Pentecost when the Holy Spirit came to the disciples who were waiting for the power, as instructed by the Lord. Obviously the experience did not end with those first disciples; it continued to be given to all those who believed, as Jesus had said it would.

Even Paul himself, after persecuting the Christians and being stopped on the Damascus road by the Lord, and after being led blind into Damascus due to this encounter with the Lord, had the laying on of hands by Ananias to receive his sight and to be filled with the Holy Spirit. There is nothing to tell us whether or not Paul immediately spoke in tongues, but we know from what he wrote himself that he had this wonderful gift. When he was encouraging and instructing the Corinthians, he said, **"I thank my God I speak with tongues more than you all,"** and **"He that speaketh in an unknown tongue edifieth himself."** He also said that **"He that speaketh in an unknown tongue speaketh not unto men but unto God,"** and that in the Spirit **"he speaketh mysteries."** He also told them that if he spoke in an unknown tongue, his spirit prayed. (1 Corinthians 14).

Paul knew the benefits of this supernatural avenue of communication with God, and he gave instruction as to its proper use, for he said that in an assembly of people it was better to prophesy, or, if there was a message in tongues it needed to be interpreted. To stand up and speak in an unknown tongue in front of an assembly would not do anything for the listeners; it is much better for them to be instructed in a language they can understand.

How we all need to be edified and to know this experience of praying with the Spirit, enabling us to be sensitive to the Lord and to His leading, helping us to walk in the Spirit and to worship God.

The Holy Spirit has been given to lead us into all truth, with the consequence that we know when we have grieved the Lord or moved wrongly. He helps us in prayer, for so often we do not know how to pray. My confidence in the leading of the Holy Spirit and in the utterances in tongues that come forth in intercession causes me to believe that intercession is being made according to the will of God.

What a comfort to be able to pray for a person or a situation under the complete guidance of the Holy Spirit. If I rush into praying with my limited understanding, asking God to do what I think should be done, I so often miss the target in prayer. On the other hand, if I take time to pray in tongues and allow the Holy Spirit to make intercession through me, that prayer is of the highest order;

and, amazingly, He often enlightens me or directs me during that time so that I know what to pray with my understanding and I know what requests to make to God.

I can be affected by knowing a few limited details concerning the situation for which I am praying or the person for whom intercession is required. Speaking in tongues helps me to get free emotionally and free in my thinking.

I can approach God concerning a matter that is far too big for my faith — beyond my reach in faith — and can pray in tongues, knowing the help of the Holy Spirit, for He brings my faith into action by a word or a vision or just an inner knowing. As I then begin to move in faith, I know that my praying in tongues is fruitful, and my faith is built up to a level where I can pray in English and know that I have prayed in faith and have touched God concerning the matter on hand.

There is so much to be discovered about this wonderful gift. Even when Paul was correcting the church at Corinth so that there should not be misuse of this gift, we learn something more about it. He was telling them that if there was no interpreter there was to be no message in tongues in the church — that the person was to keep silent and speak to himself or to God; therefore he could use the gift silently and would not disturb anyone. This must mean that we can use this gift silently anywhere, building us up and keeping us free in the midst of so much evil in this world.

Through Paul we realise that this gift is a personal one, but it is also a public ministry, because tongues with interpretation gives God's word in a similar way to prophecy. A message in tongues alerts and prepares us for what God is about to say through the interpretation.

I have also discovered that in a prayer meeting this gift can be used in united intercession, for in a prayer meeting people have not met to speak to one another or to teach one another. They have gathered together to meet God and communicate with Him, so in a united way they can speak to God in their natural tongue or in the language that the Holy Spirit has given to them. This usually comes about with a group that is in one accord and where they can all speak or pray in tongues, and it has been discovered that this has great advantage as they unite to intercede. As the Holy Spirit makes intercession through the group, their united faith brings results against the powers of darkness, proving it to be a weapon that is not carnal but mighty through God to the pulling down of strongholds. (2 Corinthians 10:4).

3

Oneness with the Leader

It was a revelation to me when I realised that it had not taken God forty years to prepare Moses to lead the Children of Israel out of Egypt. As I re-read that story one day, I realised that God had been waiting for the Children of Israel to cry unto Him, for when the Lord spoke to Moses out of the midst of the burning bush, He said, **"the cry of the children of Israel is come unto me." (Exodus 3:9).**

To think that deliverance was only a 'cry' away, and depended on their calling upon God, who was ready to act on their behalf!

I had known that as a Christian I should not only pray but ***want*** to pray and cry unto the Lord, but so much of my praying seemed ineffective, and usually I did not know how to pray. I could certainly identify myself with the familiar verse in

Romans chapter eight — at least the part which says **"we know not what we should pray for as we ought,"** but I did not understand or know in my experience the other part of that scripture **"how the Spirit itself maketh intercession for us with groanings which cannot be uttered,"** or the following verse which says that **"he maketh intercession for the saints according to the will of God."**

Adding "if it be Thy will" at the end of most of my prayers seemed to cover the matter and to come into line with that word, but more often than not I did not know what was the will of God. I concluded that, because my prayers were not answered in the way I thought or desired they should be, it was not the will of God to answer me in that way.

I could not equate my experience with what we read in 1 John 2:6, **"He that saith he abideth in him ought himself also so to walk, even as he walked."** Also in John 14:13, Jesus said, **"whatsoever ye shall ask in my name, that will I do."** Jesus knew that Father always heard Him, and that He always prayed or moved or spoke according to Father's will. How then are we to walk as He walked?

I am gradually discovering some of the depths of meaning in these familiar words. I believe that as I go step by step with the Lord, pondering not only on what He says to me, but on what I say to Him, I shall find the reality of these verses and the hidden manna which He has promised.

It was in 1969, in a meeting in the United States

of America, that the Lord asked me how much I loved Him. I was ready to answer in the same way that I had often answered my husband, by saying that I loved Him with all my heart; but before those words were silently uttered I thought, "How much is that?" I knew that I could not measure my love for the Lord, even if I said "with all my heart." I told Him that I did not know how much I loved Him, but one thing I did know, if it was possible to love Him more, then I wanted to.

He told me then how much I loved Him. He said, "You love me as much as you trust Me in every situation."

I was thrilled with those words, and a joy welled up within me because I knew then that as I trusted the Lord in every situation which was a challenge, or full of difficulties, I would go into a new depth of love for Him.

I began to see that love and trust went hand in hand. Over the years I have experienced new depths of my love for the Lord and His love for me — new depths of trusting Him and discovering that He trusts me.

A few days after that meeting in America, I was being taken by car to another State and was pondering on the fact that the Lord had asked me how much I loved Him. I had the overwhelming desire to ask Him how much He loved me, but then thought I was being presumptuous and could not ask the Lord such a question. Surely I knew that He loved me enough to die for me, and had fully given

Himself for me, but I still wanted to ask Him — for I wanted to hear Him tell me how much He loved me.

Rather hesitantly I said, "Lord, You asked me how much I loved You; I just want to ask You how much You love me?"

His reply was immediate and He said, "Enough to give you My name."

I could hardly believe my ears. This was unexpected for I had thought He would surely say "Enough to die for you."

I meditated upon His words and thought about His name, which has authoritiy over every other name in the world. I likened the heavenly marriage to the natural marriage, for when a man marries he not only gives himself to his wife but he gives her his name. The woman does not give her name to him, but she does give for she ***gives up*** her name, which means that she loses her own personal identity to become one with him.

I thought about my own marriage and how my husband was responsible for all that I did in his name. I was not born bearing his name, but I became his name when I married him. In the same way, when I entered into union with Jesus I lost my own personal identity and received His name and the authority that goes with it. His name has authority over every other name in the world, and nothing can come against it. He has given Himself to us and He has told us to do everything in His name.

I knew then that it was not just a question of praying and adding the phrase "in the name of Jesus." I knew it was not just knowing the name — but ***being*** the name.

I now no longer want to do things for myself and of myself, and as the years have gone by in this partnership with Jesus I have realised that the more I know Him to whom I am joined, the more I know the position of power and authority in His name.

Receiving His guidance, we do not pray hoping that what we pray is His will, for He reveals Himself in such a way that we can discern His will.

4

Faith Required!

As a young Christian I was not instructed to expect to hear the voice of the Lord. I thought He only spoke to the people that we read about in the Scriptures, such as Abraham, Moses, Joshua and the early disciples. Maybe a few special people today, such as prominent ministers, would also hear His voice — but not just a housewife!

After reading what Jesus said in John 10, "**My sheep hear my voice.**" and also what He said to Pilate in John 18:37, "**Everyone that is of the truth heareth my voice,**" I realised that as I belonged to the Lord and was one of His sheep, I should be able to hear His voice.

I thought about the metaphor that the Lord had used, and how sheep need to be guided and how safe they are under the guidance of a good shepherd. I considered other animals that learn to know the voice of their master, and the obedience that is meant to be established between the voice and the hearer — also the delight the master experiences in the response, as well as the safety and the guidance given to the one knowing the voice.

I talked to the Lord about these things and asked Him to teach me to know His voice. The Lord moved through my situation and my day to day activities to bring me into this experience.

I had kept a particular matter hidden from my mother, thinking it was best for her, but after a time this began to weigh heavily upon me. I poured out my heart to the Lord, telling Him that I wanted to be right in His sight and right before my mother. He then spoke to me and showed me what to do, giving clear instructions so that the whole matter might be brought into the light where the enemy could not use it.

His voice to me at that time was like an audible voice, because it did not come from within me; it was outside of me. I looked around the room, expecting to see God, for the voice and the instructions were so clear. He told me to go and tell my mother all things from the beginning, and He would see that she would receive them. Not only did I obey, but I proved that God kept His word. The whole matter was brought into the light and I was right before God and before my mother.

I had been thrilled that God had spoken to me in such a clear way, and I told Him that if He would continue to speak to me so clearly He would have my full obedience; whatever He asked me to do, I would do it. I had felt elated at the thought that I had joined the ranks of those who had not only heard the voice of the Lord but had had clear instructions concerning what they were to do.

The frustrating part was that God did not speak to me again in this manner. After a few days had gone by I reminded Him of my promise that I would do whatever He asked of me. Still no word came from the Lord! Once more I talked to Him, and said, "Lord, I have tasted something so wonderful and I just want to hear You speaking to me. You talked to Adam and Eve in the cool of the evening; they knew Your voice and enjoyed Your presence, and I want to continue hearing Your voice, Lord. Please speak to me again." And still the Lord remained silent.

More time went by and I talked to Him again about this matter. I said, "Lord, You surely would not give me a taste for something and then withhold it from me — like dangling a carrot before my eyes and yet keeping it out of reach. Please speak to me again, Lord, and tell me what You would have me do." No sound came, and God remained silent!

Then, in my frustration, I said to Him one day, "If You are never going to speak to me again, I would rather You had not spoken to me at all. Surely You would not speak to me once in my lifetime and then leave me without another word for the rest of my life."

Still no word came from the Lord, and, because I had not been able to make Him speak to me and He had not answered my cry, I began to ponder in my heart why this should be so. Why was He willing to speak to me once in a clear voice and then not speak to me again? I knew I meant what I had said to the Lord concerning my willingness to obey. What could be the reason for His silence?

I then began to believe that He had a very good reason for being silent, and the words that came to my mind were **"The just shall live by faith."**

"Oh, I see, Lord. If You always spoke to me in an audible voice I would not have to use my faith, for it requires no faith to hear an audible voice, but it does require faith to hear Your still small voice that comes from within."

I realised that I was about to begin a new walk with the Lord — a walk of faith, where I would have to believe that I was hearing His voice, a walk that would cause me to begin to listen. How would I know the difference between His voice and my own thoughts? How would I know the difference concerning my own good ideas and His guidance? I realised that there was only one way to find out, and that was to prove for myself His voice and His guidance, to begin to learn what it meant to be led by the Holy Spirit.

I was about to discover that His voice within me was so like my own thoughts that I often had to pluck up courage to believe that the Lord was speaking to me and that it was not my own thinking. The voice of the Lord is so personal that I can mistake Him for me or me for Him.

This I have done, for I have made mistakes, and my mistakes have usually come about when I have been trying to push my own good ideas without first talking to the Lord and taking the time to give Him an opportunity to guide me.

The Lord then took me through a number of experiences which helped me to become confident in my fellowship with Him. He spoke to me in one meeting, telling me to give just a small amount of money to a young woman who was there. It seemed like my own thought, but I gave her the money. She said, "Praise the Lord, it is just what I need for my bus fare."

On another occasion, while I was combing my hair and getting myself ready for a meeting one Sunday morning, I said to the Lord, "Do You want to show me anything for the meeting? Do You want me to give anything?"

Immediately He answered, "Give one pound to . . . ," and He gave me the name of a nurse who sometimes came to the meetings when she was off duty.

I was a little troubled because over the previous weeks, whenever I had asked the Lord how much money I should give to various collections or to people, it had always been one pound. I had begun to wonder whether or not I was hearing properly from the Lord, or whether I was limiting Him.

I thought perhaps there was something in me

that did not want to give more than one pound, and so I said to the Lord, "Am I really hearing aright? I do not want to limit You with my thinking."

He replied, "All right, give two pounds."

"Well," I thought, "what is this all about?" I obeyed, realising that I was still learning to hear the voice of the Lord.

At the end of the meeting I went to another room where I had left my handbag, to take out the two pounds to give to that nurse. I turned round and discovered that she had followed me into the room. She held out her hand with something concealed in it, and said, "The Lord has told me to give you this."

I was puzzled, but extended my hand to her with the two pounds concealed in it, and said, "But the Lord has told me to give this to you."

We exchanged what was in our hands and I was so amazed at what the Lord had done. He had told her to give me one pound, which meant that while I was handing her two pounds, I had in fact only given one pound, which was the amount that He had first told me to give. I shared with the nurse my conversation with the Lord, and we laughed at the way He was teaching me. I was thrilled that I had heard Him aright and that I was not limiting Him by my own thinking.

Another delightful experience of learning to hear the voice of the Lord took place when I was helping at a Christian holiday camp for children.

The oven had only two shelves, and I knew that we would need three in order to cater adequately for the numbers at that camp. Apart from the oven there was only a double-ring gas burner in the kitchen.

The first time we needed to use three shelves, I said to the Lord, "Whatever can I do, Lord, for I cannot put everything on two shelves?"

"Take the top off the double gas burner," He replied.

I did as the Lord had said, and carried it to the oven. I was wide-eyed with amazement and delight as I slid the 'shelf' into position. Not only did it have to be the right width, but it had to be the right thickness, for there were grooves in the sides of the oven into which the shelves lodged. Only the Lord knew how to provide an extra shelf incorporating two different pieces of equipment by two different makers.

How wonderful that He can speak to us and that we can hear His instructions.

I also discovered that 'picture language' can often convey more than words alone. Sometimes it is easier for the Lord to give me a picture upon which I can meditate than to speak directly with words.

These pictures I call 'visions', but I could also say

that the Holy Spirit uses my imagination or that in my mind's eye I see a picture.

In prayer one day concerning a meeting which was to take place in my home, I visualised the people who would be there. I saw them sitting on the various chairs in the room, and then it was as if I could see Jesus standing in the middle of the room. As I looked, I could no longer see Jesus but a tree trunk. I then saw branches of the tree appear, which reached out and bent over and touched each chair. As the branches touched the chairs I could no longer see the people but only the branches of the tree.

Of course I knew the word which the Lord was lighting up to me about Himself being the vine and we the branches. This vision, or this picture, helped me to lose sight of the various individuals and their own particular characters and problems and their various stages of growth. I could see Jesus — not only in the centre of the meeting but in them. I also became aware that we are all equal in His sight, and that not one of us can reckon ourselves special above anyone else. Our life comes from Him and in a meeting our eyes are not to be upon each other but upon Him.

On another occasion a minister telephoned me at ten o'clock one evening and asked me to pray, for he needed a word from the Lord. He did not enlighten me as to why this was important, but asked me to telephone him within fifteen minutes if the Lord showed me anything.

Immediately I knelt down and prayed, and the Lord used the wonderful avenue of picture language to give me His word. I saw the moon and stars in the night sky, and the Lord reminded me of the story of Joseph and his dream of the stars bowing down before him. Then, as I waited on the Lord, He said, "The details of the situation must bow to My authority in this minister."

I telephoned and gave him the word of the Lord, for which he thanked me, again without enlightening me concerning any of the details.

About one year later, when I met him and his wife, he gave me a few details of that situation. They had had someone staying in their home whom they were trying to help, and they had found her on the floor in the bedroom either deeply drugged or unconscious; beside her was an empty bottle from which tablets had been taken.

They had prayed over her and had listened to the Lord, who had told them to lift her on to the bed and to leave her for the night. They had followed the instructions but wanted to doubly check that they were hearing aright.

The vision and the word assured them of His instructions and that their prayer of authority was backed by the power of God.

The Lord has spoken to me in many ways — through an advertisement on a hoarding, or in some simple way through part of His creation such as a bird flying in the sky or the sea pounding upon the rocks on the beach.

His voice can even be an inner knowing that does not require words or pictures. We can intuitively know what is required of us — what to say, what to do or where to go.

I experienced my first lesson concerning this when I was seeking the Lord about a decision I had to make which involved a choice between two things and which had to be made known on a certain day.

About two weeks beforehand, I asked the Lord to direct me and told Him that He would know the best choice to make. He did not speak to me on that occasion and, knowing that there was plenty of time for Him to show me, I did not pursue the matter.

A week before the deadline date, I asked the Lord again to make clear to me which was the best decision. He remained silent and I wondered why He did not tell me. I did not think too much about it, in fact I believe I shrugged my shoulders and thought, "I must ask Him again nearer the time."

Two days before the particular day of decision I asked for His help and direction, adding that I only wanted to choose what was in line with His choice and His decision, and would He please make it clear to me either by a word or a vision. Again no answer came.

I enquired of Him the next day, getting on my

knees in a deliberate action of showing that I really was seeking Him and was not treating the matter casually. I rose from my knees, and thought, "I will ask Him again in the morning." This I did, repeating my desire to please Him, and wanting His direction.

He remained silent, so I then said, "Well, Lord, You know that I have to give my decision today. I cannot put it off, I shall just have to make a choice. I would like You to have directed me, but You cannot say that I did not ask You!"

So I simply took time to think about the matter on hand and made a decision. I was amazed at the way the Lord confirmed to me that I had made the right choice. He seemed to go to extra trouble to show me in different ways that I had done the right thing.

I said to Him, "I don't understand You, Lord. I kept talking to You about this matter, telling You that I wanted Your help and Your guidance, and now You go to all this trouble to confirm that I did the right thing. Why, Lord?"

I sat in silence with the Lord, and slowly began to see what He was teaching me. I said, "Do You really want me to believe that I am one with You, and can make decisions and choices out of that oneness, and my choice will be Yours, and Your choice mine?"

I love the Lord for the way that He so gently leads us on. He is the perfect teacher and the perfect guide. All He requires are willing committed pupils.

5

Being Committed

I had no idea that learning to hear and recognise the voice of the Lord would mean a development in prayer. Prayer was always something that seemed mystical and out of reach, that only a selected few seemed to achieve with satisfaction. The level of prayer that I had found in my early years of being a Christian did not satisfy me, and because of that I did not pursue it, but left it to devote my time to more gratifying avenues of service.

There was a particular time when someone asked me if I had read "Rees Howells Intercessor." I had not even heard of it, but listened to the recommendation that it was a wonderful book on prayer. I made my way to the Christian bookshop and, having found the book, I opened it somewhere in the middle and read a small portion.

I hastily put it down, thinking in no way did I want to read that book. The little portion I had read of Rees Howells' experience seemed too hard, and called for a rigorous life of hardship.

Amazingly, over the next few weeks a number of people asked me if I had read that book. I would immediately shake my head "No," but secretly thinking "and I am not going to read it either!" It certainly did not occur to me that the Lord was moving those people to ask me that question, and only now can I see His purpose for doing so, for He was requiring a response from me. He was seeking a commitment from me, for, as I reflect back on what I said to Him, I now realise that it was what He was wanting to hear.

After being asked a number of times if I had read the book, and inwardly refusing to do so, I did eventually talk to the Lord about it. I told Him that I did not want to read about intercession and said truthfully that it did not appeal to me, but because I had chosen to give my life completely to Him and I only wanted to fulfil His will for me, if He wanted me to be involved in intercession He would have to take me into it.

I was willing for Him to do that, but I was not going to try to get into it by reading about someone else's experience. I was very definite in what I said to the Lord, but I had no idea that that was just what He was desiring of me — a willingness to be taken into intercession — almost as if we give Him permission to do something in our lives!

On another occasion and while praying in tongues one day, I suddenly stopped and said to the

Lord, "Do you want to show me another country to which You want me to go?"

Immediately He answered, "India."

It was a complete shock to me; I almost wished I had not asked Him because I had never had any interest in that country and certainly no desire to go there. I did not know any missionaries involved in the work in India, neither had I been interested enough to read or to enquire about any outreach to that country.

I said to the Lord, "If You really want me to go to India, and if it is Your will and purpose for me then I am willing, Lord; but You must work it out, giving me the right contacts and showing me when I am to go."

I had committed myself once again in response to the Lord. The fact that I did not go to India until seven years later is by the way; my going was the result of my response and what I had replied to the Lord.

On another occasion, about midnight and at the end of a very busy day, I made a different commitment to the Lord. There were a number of things about which I needed to pray, and, as I climbed into bed, I said to the Lord, "If You wake me up early I will get up and pray."

I think I fell asleep as soon as my head touched the pillow, and much later I was roused, or perhaps I can say became semi-conscious. As I began to change my position, the words came to me, "If You wake me up early I will get up and pray."

I groaned within, for I was warm and cosy in bed and my body was still tired and I needed more sleep. I knew that I only had to change my position and I would be blissfully unconscious again. I did not want to get up, and had no desire to pray, but I had said I would if the Lord woke me. I had committed myself and I knew that I must follow it through.

I believe it is very important that we keep our word. We must mean what we say. We expect God to keep His word — He expects us to keep ours.

So, with my eyes still closed, I sat upright in bed and slowly made myself emerge into the cold dark morning. It was at the time of the year when it was still dark at the usual time of waking. I knew that I had to get out of my bedroom, away from the temptation of the bed. I groped my way downstairs and was dismayed when I looked at my watch to see that it was only four o'clock in the morning.

However, I believed that the Lord had woken me, but I thought, "if I kneel down I shall go to sleep on my knees, and unless I take deliberate action to keep myself awake, there will be nothing done through my rising early."

I started right away to speak in tongues, and immediately became wide-awake. All tiredness left my body — in fact I felt full of vitality and strength.

I stopped praying in tongues and said, "Lord, You are crafty!" I did not mean that disrespectfully; it was my expression of surprise at the way He had woken me, for He had only given me a little nudge. I had expected Him, if He was going to wake me, to make a good job of it, but in His wisdom and skilful training He had answered my prayer, but not in the way I had anticipated. He had roused me only sufficiently to see whether or not I would go past all my natural feelings and keep my word, whether my commitment to Him came first rather than my natural desires. But as soon as He had seen my word fulfilled, He came to me with the fulfilment of His promise that those who wait upon the Lord shall renew their strength. (Isaiah 40:31).

I had never seen the full value of that promise or the real meaning, and I can honestly say that my strength was renewed that morning in prayer and the few hours of sleep I had that night were adequate. Not only was my strength renewed but I had a most precious time with the Lord, knowing His presence, receiving guidance and having my faith quickened to believe for various solutions concerning a number of situations and problems for which I was praying.

There is a world of difference between waiting *for* the Lord and waiting *upon* Him. Waiting *for* the Lord is a trap into which I have fallen so many times, for I have been looking for Him to do something when all the time He has been wanting me to seek Him, or to ask the right question, or even waiting for me to say I was sorry about some incident which needed my repentance.

There are promises He has made to us and for which we have no need to wait, for His promises are to be believed and acted upon. Faith lays hold of God's word and does not wait for God to produce the evidence before believing.

Waiting ***upon*** God is different, for we must wait upon Him to know what He requires of us and to discern His will. Waiting upon Him shows Him our willingness to obey, and gives Him the opportunity to speak and direct us. Waiting upon Him gives us confidence and satisfaction and we accumulate insight and revelation which cannot be received in any other way.

I have discovered that my commitment to my brothers and sisters is, in God's sight, equally as important as my commitment to Him.

A certain minister was to accompany a group of Christians who were going to Israel for a holiday. He would have led the worship and prayer time each day, but at the last minute he was unable to go. I was asked to take his place and accompany the group.

I knew a sense of excitement at the invitation, for I was looking forward to my first visit to Israel. As I talked to the Lord about it, He reminded me of a commitment I had made to spend a day with a Christian woman who not only needed fellowship but needed encouragement concerning the difficulties and problems in her life.

Immediately I thought I could postpone my visit, and see her upon my return from Israel, but I was plagued with the thought that I would not be fulfilling my commitment. I knew I had to walk uprightly in this situation and decline the invitation to Israel in order to keep my word to one of God's children.

The Lord also showed me that this was doubly important because the woman had an insecure background and had not really trusted anyone. I could see how the Lord was trying to give to her in order that she might put her trust completely in Him and also begin to trust members of the Body of Christ.

Other changes have taken place in my life, and have been determined by what I have said to the Lord. He has taken my words and because of them has given me new experiences, new challenges and new insight, so that little by little He is transforming me into His image. This transforming process takes us into a place where we desire what He desires and even think in oneness with Him.

6

An Obscured View

Learning to walk in the Spirit and receiving directions from the Lord does not always mean that we see the goal which the Lord has in mind. He may give us a word, or show us something that He wants us to do, but our limited minds prevent us from seeing the full outcome of the instructions He has given us.

The Lord moved through a desire I once had, and in spite of my not being able to see His goal or the outcome of my walk of faith, He was able to direct me away from ***my*** goal to His.

I had the strong desire to move into a larger house, for my three-bedroom semi-detached had become overcrowded and I wanted to give more comfort to my own family as well as having accommodation available for the people that God kept sending to me.

I prayed and asked the Lord for a larger house, and then started the process of searching for the right one. During that period of time I asked the Lord to give me a word to confirm that I was right in looking for another house, and I received the verse in 1 Chronicles 28, saying, **"For the Lord hath chosen thee to build an house for the sanctuary, be strong and do it."**

I took this as my confirming word to go ahead with buying and moving into a larger house. I registered at all the well-known estate agents, and was continually receiving details of properties and looking at those which I thought most suitable.

This went on for a long time, and I began to get weary of looking, not even bothering to look at the details of houses for sale as they came through the post. Later I sought the Lord again, and asked Him if He still wanted me to hold the word for a house. I began to wonder if I had really heard correctly, and told Him that I was more than willing to lay it all aside if I had made a mistake, or if for any reason His plans had been changed.

The Lord answered, and said very clearly, "I want you to continue to hold My word."

I entered into a new stage of peace, where I no longer rushed around looking at properties; a peace which kept me from trying to work out how I would be able to make a purchase, or imagining ways in which God could give me a different property.

Answering the telephone one day, I was amazed when a lady's voice enquired, "Is that Mrs. Flude?" On my reply, she gave her name, and said, "You do not know me but are you in need of any money?"

I was speechless, for I had never been asked such a question by a complete stranger over the telephone! Before I could gather my wits, or make any reply, she went on to tell me that she had sold a piece of land and had been asking the Lord what He would have her do with the money, and the Lord had given her one word — 'Ipswich'.

She did not know anyone in Ipswich and had spent many days wondering what to do until she remembered that she had a book which contained my name and address, and had then made the decision to telephone me.

I explained to her how I had been looking to the Lord for money in order to purchase a larger house, and suggested that it would be good for us to meet and share together.

Her husband kindly drove many miles to bring her to my home and the outcome, after our meeting and mutual agreement to wait on the Lord concerning the details, was that the Lord directed her to loan me a fairly large sum of money interest-free for ten years.

By the time this had all taken place, the cost of houses had rocketed, and where the money available could have been a very good deposit on a large house, it would then only be sufficient for a deposit on a small one.

Later on I shared these details with a friend who was visiting me, and after a few days she said, "I have been praying about what you have shared concerning another house, and I believe the Lord wants me to write a letter to someone I know personally who I am sure would be thrilled to loan some money on the same basis."

To my amazement, the Lord opened the door for another large sum of money to be made available on loan interest free by this unknown person via my friend. I kept asking the Lord to show me what to do, because I knew that the money then available was hardly sufficient to buy a small house.

The more I prayed and looked at different properties, the more I felt that the money was to be used for a small house and not a large one. I could not understand it; I did not think that the Lord wanted me to move from one small house to another. The only way I could reason it out was by thinking that an additional house would ease the situation, although it did not seem practical to run two houses.

My lack of understanding did not prevent me from going forward. I began looking at small houses, but because I had no vision for a small house, nothing seemed right. I remained in peace even though there was money available for use and I still did not know what to do with it.

The Lord in His own wonderful way directed me one morning to pray for a minister whom I had known for a number of years and showed me that he and his wife and children would be moving.

A few weeks later, while praying for that family again, the Lord revealed to me that they would be coming to Ipswich and that the word for the house and the money that had been made available was His provision for them. This was so clear, and the pieces of the jigsaw which I had held in my hand and which I had been unable to fit together were now falling into place by the Spirit of God. He gave me understanding at the right time.

The word I had received from God and my desire to have a larger house had been used of Him, although my interpretation and and my ideas of moving had not been right. God had used it all, and I had the privilege of being trusted by the Lord with His word and with the money.

Eventually the Lord was able to make a way for that man to purchase the house for himself, and the money on loan for God's use was returned.

There was just one question left in my mind — why I had taken so long to see what God had meant concerning my desire and the word that He had given to me. I so often knew what the Lord required of me and moved in the right direction, but in this instance I had gone round and round in circles. I asked the Lord to show me something about this and why I had been so slow to discern His will concerning the house.

One day, as I made my way to a hospital eight miles from Ipswich to visit my husband, my attention was suddenly attracted to a shimmering glittering mass in the clear blue sky in the distance ahead of me.

I had never seen anything like it before. It seemed as if there were diamonds hanging in the sky. As I drew nearer, I began to realise that this glittering mass was moving and that it was a flock of birds. The sun shining upon their wings had given this unusual phenomenon, and I knew that through it the Lord was saying something to me.

I guessed then that they were probably pigeons, and as I turned off the main road I saw two men putting cages back into a vehicle parked along the country lane. I wanted to stop and watch, but travelled on because I knew that I was late for the visiting time at the hospital.

I was so impressed by the scene, and the way my attention had been drawn to those birds, that I asked the Lord several times what He was saying to me through this visual aid.

I made the journey to the hospital each day, and exactly a week later as I turned off the main road I had to pull up quickly, because the two men were there letting the pigeons out of the cages again. The birds were flying across the road before soaring into the sky, which meant that I had to stop. As I stepped from my car I was determined to find out what the Lord wanted to say to me.

I watched the birds coming together in the sky and beginning to circle round the area. I said to one of the men, "Didn't I see you letting these pigeons out about a week ago?"

"Oh, yes," he replied, "we are just giving them some practice flights."

I asked him how far they had to fly.

"About forty-five miles," he replied, "they will be home before we are."

I expressed my admiration to him concerning those birds and how they were able to find their way. I stood with him watching and asked how long they flew round in a circle.

"Well, it varies," he answered. "Sometimes they go straight up and straight off in the direction they have to take; there is no hesitation and they know which way to go. Other times they will circle round for about ten minutes or more before they get their bearings, and before they know which way to head."

I was thrilled. God had answered my question through that man and the pigeons. I stood and watched them until they finally knew which way to go and disappeared out of sight.

Many times God had spoken to me and I had known what to do, but on this issue it seemed that I had taken such a long time to get my bearings. The

Lord was showing me that while it appeared that I had gone round in a circle, it was right that I had done so, for while I was moving I could get my direction.

I could see that if those pigeons had sat on the fence, or had not soared into the sky and flown round, they would never have got their bearings and would never have headed home. I realised then that we must keep moving, even if we are not always sure of the direction in which to go. God will guide our steps and show us the way He would have us take, even if we do not understand. Seeing a goal had caused me to soar and fly, and only when flying could I be directed to God's goal.

7

Learning Obedience

My journey with the Lord has led me to discover not only His love, His life and His power, but details about myself and how my self-life can rule me.

One day I decided to do something, and I knew that if I talked to the Lord about the matter I would not be able to do it. It was not that what I was going to do was sinful in itself; I just knew that He would rather I did not take that particular action, so I did not talk to Him, and deliberately turned from Him to do that which I had purposed to do. Afterwards, however, I knew a grief within myself, for how could I have fellowship with the Lord without being distressed that my own selfish life had had the pre-eminence. I wept and told the Lord that I was sorry I had gone on my own way.

Some weeks previously I had told Him I was going to believe that I was walking in oneness with

Him; now, as I poured out my heart, I said, "How can I ever believe that I am in oneness with You when I continue to go my own way?"

He gave me a vision of a circle drawn on the ground, and I knew it represented holy ground. I had been standing upon that holy ground but, because of my own selfish desire and my action, I had stepped off it.

Through my tears, I said, "Lord, how can I get back on to that holy ground?"

He answered, "He that is clean needeth not to be washed save his feet only."

I then remembered that on one occasion I had asked the Lord a question concerning the incident when He had washed the disciples' feet. Peter said to Him, **"You shall never wash my feet"** and the Lord answered, **"If I wash thee not, thou hast no part with me."** Peter then replied, **"Not my feet only, but also my hands and my head,"** and the Lord said, **"He that is washed needeth not save to wash his feet, but is clean every whit." (John 13).**

I had told the Lord that I did not understand what He meant by that statement, and now He was showing me. I was clean, I had not lost my robe of righteousness, but I had stepped on to ground that had soiled my feet, and my feet needed to be washed. I thanked Him, and knew that it was an act of faith on my part that I let Him wash my feet and, by a further act of faith, I stepped back on to the holy ground where I had been in oneness with Him.

This was not my only experience of going my own way and spoiling my fellowship with the Lord, for while travelling in Denmark with my invalid husband and a friend I again fell into a similar trap, when the Lord spoke to me and showed me something that I should not do. I heard Him but did not think about His words or respond to carry out His will; I still went my own way, and so, in His love, He had to correct me and show me my lack of response to Him.

I had been to the laundry room on the camp site with a load of washing which needed to be done for my invalid husband. Because of the rainy weather, I knew I had to find a launderette somewhere in the local town where I could get the linen spun and dried.

After reaching the launderette and putting the linen in the drier, I lifted my wrist to look at my watch, only to discover that I had left it in the laundry room on the camp site. I immediately prayed and asked the Lord to look after it, for I knew that He could keep it protected for me. It was the last gift I had received from my husband before he had been taken seriously ill; it had kept perfect time and, as well as being of practical value to me, it also had sentimental value.

I believed that the Lord would look after my watch for me, and on my return to the camp site went straight to the laundry room to collect it — but discovered that it had been removed. Immediately I thought that someone must have taken it to the office and I made my way there, only to learn that it had not been handed in.

We had planned to leave the next morning and I again went to the office, expecting to receive my watch. I was dismayed when the man indicated that it had not been given to him, adding, "It is very unlikely for a watch to be handed in."

I knew that the Lord could have protected my wristwatch, and so I enquired of Him, "Lord, why did You not look after my watch for me? I know that You could have hidden it from the eyes of everyone who went into that laundry room."

Immediately He showed me that I had not paid any attention to the word that He had spoken to me. In order for our oneness to continue He had deliberately taken action, and had done with my word what I had done with His — He had ignored it!

While I was sorry concerning the loss of my watch, I was thankful to the Lord that He could correct me so quickly and would take steps to prevent my going astray from Him. I told Him I was sorry I had ignored His word, and was even glad that He could take my wristwatch in order to measure out that correction to me. I also told the Lord I would be content without one until He found a way to give me another.

Only about two weeks had gone by when the Lord in His wonderful way moved upon a young man to give me a watch almost identical to the one I had lost. That young man had no idea of what the Lord had been doing in my life, and that he was His instrument in restoring me to my faith walk of oneness.

We can make determined efforts to follow after the Lord, and the greatest delight of all is discovering that little by little and step by step He is bringing us into oneness with Himself.

8

Gaining Experience

To become effective pray-ers, we must learn to be good listeners. Learning to listen to the voice of the Holy Spirit within us means we must take time to wait upon the Lord. Our soulish realm can be so active of itself and, indeed, before we were made alive in our spirits and became new creatures by the precious blood of Jesus, we had functioned only by the avenue of our five senses — what we see, what we hear, what we feel, what we taste and what we touch — by all the information that comes to us and affects us in our souls. This was the way that we lived and operated.

When we become new creatures in Christ Jesus and the Holy Spirit takes up His abode deep within us, we have to learn to function in a completely different way. It is not that our souls become inactive, but they have to come into subjection to the life of the Spirit of God within us.

We need to experience a deep inner spiritual relationship with Christ. We need to know how our restless souls can be quietened, in order to sense the direction and the all-pervading power of the Spirit of God within us. If only I had realised this when I first became a Christian, what a difference there would have been in my life and in my testimony.

The Lord said, in Matthew 13 verse 44, **"The kingdom of heaven is like unto treasure hid in a field; the which when a man has found, he hideth, and for joy thereof goeth and selleth all that he hath, and buyeth that field."** To know and experience that deep inner fellowship with the Lord is like discovering treasure hidden in a field.

I do not have to go anywhere to find the Lord; He is within me. I only have to practise letting the life of the Lord have the pre-eminence. My soul, which includes my emotions and my feelings, is fed by my five senses and my activities are motivated by the soulish realm. We need to take the time to allow our souls to become still so that we can be energised or motivated by the Holy Spirit.

As I look back, I realise that so often I have prayed without taking the time to allow my soul to become still, particularly when praying for members of my own family. To see them in need or hurt, or in any challenge or dilemma, affects my feelings, and too often I have rushed to pray because I am emotionally involved.

When my younger daughter and her husband

decided to go to Germany in March, my natural motherly instinct had the pre-eminence over my thinking and praying. At the time of the journey she would be five-and-a-half months pregnant, and when she told me that they would be travelling by ship my mind went into action. March winds are a part of our English heritage, and the North Sea is often affected by them. I imagined gale-force winds with high seas, and the ship on which she would be travelling reeling and rolling in tumultuous waves.

Fears for the safety of the unborn child, even thoughts of a miscarriage and my daughter being in a dilemma on that journey, robbed me of my peace of mind. Endeavouring to show a calmness, which I did not feel, I said to my daughter, "Are you sure you are doing right to go by ship? Wouldn't it be better to fly?"

She replied, "I think it will be all right, Mum."

Left on my own with my wandering thoughts, I prayed and told the Lord that I thought it would be much better if they flew, and would He cause them to see that.

When I saw my daughter again, about ten days later, she said, "Mum, we are going to fly to Germany now."

I inwardly thought "Praise the Lord" — until she added "in a six-seater plane."

"A six-seater plane!", I declared.

She went on, "Yes, we know someone who owns a plane and he has offered to take us."

I groaned inwardly and said to the Lord, "I would much rather they went by ship than on a six-seater plane. Can You not stop them from going altogether? I believe You can shut the door."

My mind continued working, my emotions and my love for my daughter took over, and I prayed out of my thinking and feelings instead of waiting upon the Lord or seeking Him to discern what to pray under the guidance of the Holy Spirit.

The weather was bad on the day they were due to depart, with high winds and rain. In the early evening I had a telephone call from the husband of another couple who were making the same journey. My daughter had asked him to explain that they could not go on the six-seater plane because the weather conditions were too bad for landing in Germany and the flight had had to be cancelled.

However, my daughter and her husband had left immediately for Heathrow Airport, in the hope of getting on a normal flight from there.

This man said that he and his wife were taking the circumstances as evidence that the Lord was closing the door to their going. I thought, "Why couldn't my son-in-law see that the Lord was closing the door for them too?"

I prayed again, and said, "Lord, You can still

shut the door to prevent their going."

The next morning I had another telephone call, decided, after setting out, not to go to London the previous evening, but to endeavour to go by ship from Felixstowe that morning.

I knew the sea would be rough because of the high winds, but I also knew that I could not express my concern. Again I said to the Lord, "You can still shut the door, Lord," and was expecting either to see them or have a call to say that they could not get a placc on the boat.

After five days, and on their return journey, they visited my home. They were in fine form and had obviously had a good time, with no ill effects from the journeys upon my daughter.

I was pleased to see them, and thrilled that the Lord had undertaken for them and had protected them in every way. It was obvious from their conversation that they had been blessed, for they had been to a Full Gospel Businessmen's Conference — the main object of their visit to Germany — and I knew deep down that they would have prayed about it.

Later, when talking to the Lord, I said, "I know that what I said to You was because of my emotional concern and my anxious fears, but if it was Your will for them to go, why was there so much lined up against their going?"

The Lord said that the enemy had used the situation to try to wear *me* down. They had gone through difficulties because I was walking carnally and not spiritually. The enemy knows our vulnerable areas and will do all he can to take the ground from under our feet by concentrated attacks on those areas.

I knew then that I had to be on my guard, particularly where my family was concerned, so that they would not have to go through difficulties and trials because of my emotional feelings and wrong thinking or my lack of seeking the Lord.

On another occasion I discovered how different things could be if I took the time to listen to the Lord. I had telephoned my elder daughter, and as soon as she answered she burst into tears. I tried to persuade her to share what was troubling her, but she was very distressed and said she had been challenged in so many ways and she knew the enemy was giving her a hard time. We could not have much conversation because of her crying.

I have known the time when I would have gone to her immediately to try to comfort her or to attempt to do something to help in the situation, simply because I could not bear to see her upset and did not want her to remain in that condition. On that occasion I replaced the telephone receiver and dropped to my knees to be quiet before the Lord and to seek His face on her behalf.

By doing this, my thoughts stopped racing and my emotions came under control. In other words, I believe I became still — not just physically but still in my soul and in my thinking.

After a short time I decided that I would carry out what I had originally planned for that afternoon, which was to go into town and do some shopping. I took my time and did not rush, only wanting to be sensitive to the Lord as to whether or not I was to go to my daughter.

When I returned after about two hours, I somehow knew within myself that I was free to visit her. I was calm and composed, believing that the Lord and I were one in going to her.

On my arrival she immediately burst into tears again and started to share about the onslaught that had been coming to her — thoughts that she was not really needed in the fellowship, that she would never be much use, in fact a whole list of negative things from which she could not get free.

As she related the details of this pressure and attack upon her I took paper and pencil and started to write. She thought I was listing all that the enemy had said, but instead I was writing the opposite. Satan is the father of lies and no truth abides in him (John 8:44). When he speaks he does not speak the truth, so we can know the truth even by the lies of Satan.

I then proceeded to read out the truth, and the truth set her free. As I prayed with her I knew an anointing upon that prayer and I prophesied the word of God into her life and into the situation.

I have never seen anyone lifted up so quickly. This seemed to mark a very real change in her life and I was so glad that I had not rushed to her side when she first telephoned. I was thankful that I had taken the time to let my own emotions be still, so that I could minister the life of the Lord — meeting her need and bringing her out of the conflict and imprisonment which could have been hers for many days.

To let the Lord reign in my life I must not only die to myself and my own efforts, but I must take the time to be still, emotionally and mentally, to know His divine guidance. Union with Him is my heart's desire, where I feel what He is feeling and speak what He is saying — in other words, where I am motivated by His presence deep within me, making me complete in Him.

9

Determined Effort

Even with the full intention of being a good pray-er I have often found myself confronted with the battle of mind-wandering. Changing my position to kneeling instead of sitting, or changing my location from one room to another, or to being in the car in the country instead of in the house does not stop the problem. Unfortunately, whatever position or location we may be in, we still have our minds with us and it is a personal battle that has to be won by each individual.

I have been amazed at the undisciplined wanderings of my mind, and how it has been ready to take over when I have determinedly purposed in my heart to seek the Lord in prayer. I would think of household goods that need to be added to my shopping list, a hair appointment that requires to be made, a friend to be telephoned or household duties that require attention, etc.

There have been times when I have been able deliberately and successfully to push these things from my mind, but on other occasions this has not been possible. Sometimes I have kept a notepad and pencil beside me to write down the things I needed to remember and which were preventing my mind from being still. I have even interrupted my praying to make a telephone call because I have not been able to push it away from my thinking. Some of these battles are heightened by the fact that I feel there is not much time to pray because so many jobs are demanding attention.

I had a new awakening to the power of the Word of God whcn on onc occasion I just could not battlc through all my mind-wandering. My efforts to deal with it came to nought, and in desperation I asked the Lord what to do. He said, "Read a portion of Scripture."

I opened my Bible at random and read the first chapter upon which my eyes focused and then went back to praying. It was a miracle, for my mind had become still and I was free to pray. I had not particularly noted any verse or stopped to meditate upon the chapter — I had simply read through it and it had washed me and set me free.

Another way of entering into prayer, which deals with mind-wandering, is to read a chapter of Scripture until the Holy Spirit lights up a verse or one sentence or story, then to take the time to meditate upon that which has been quickened by the Holy Spirit and to begin to pray about it.

I have often used the Psalms to take me into prayer; for instance, just to read the words of David when he said, **"The Lord is my light and my salvation; whom shall I fear? the Lord is the strength of my life; of whom shall I be afraid? (Psalm 27:1).**

This leads me easily into a prayer of thanksgiving and praise that deals with fears and misgivings that are lurking in my thoughts. This verse would probably prompt me to pray:

> "Oh, Lord, You are my light, without You I would be in darkness, without You I would not know which way to walk. You have given me light and life, You are my salvation. You have not only redeemed me and saved me from sin but You continually save me day by day by Your light. Who is there to fear when I have You, Lord? You are the God of the whole earth, the Creator, the mighty God, and You are my Lord, my Saviour and my Friend. Yes, Lord, You are the strength of my life and there is nothing of which I need to be afraid, for Your power is over and above every other power or force in this world, and in You I am strong. I just want to be Your vessel, showing forth Your light this day and the joy of Your salvation."

I could so easily continue from there requesting light and strength from the Lord concerning any matter that might be upon my heart. It is wonderful to be led in prayer by the Holy Spirit and there is no fixed pattern because our praying is a personal expression of ourselves to God.

I have found that another way of entering into prayer and dealing with the problem of mind-wandering is to take the time to write my own message to the Lord or to write my own psalm. Expression of my heart in this way helps me to concentrate on the Lord, stills my wandering mind and leaves me free to praise, to worship, to adore, to request and to intercede; in other words, I find a place where I am still — knowing God.

I have discovered that there is another side of the coin concerning my mind, for it is an avenue through which the Holy Spirit can flow. Having been stilled from its own proud and independent function, my mind can then be used by the Holy Spirit. He can bring to mind some act or word wrongly spoken, and which requires my attention before the Lord; He can use my mind for visions and for His own creative purposes, also He can remind me of the things for which I am to pray once my mind has come into subjection to the Holy Spirit by my determined effort to be fruitful in prayer.

10

Adequate Provision

Jesus said, **"Blessed are they which do hunger and thirst after righteousness: for they shall be filled." (Matt. 5:6).**

Because I wanted to be filled, I asked the Lord how I could become more spiritually hungry and thirsty. He took the natural to show me the spiritual. If I go for a while without a drink, my natural senses tell me that I need one; also, when it is getting near to a mealtime my stomach begins to tell me that I am hungry.

He also showed me that if we fast from food long enough, we reach the point where there is no desire for food. The stomach and digestive system go to sleep, and in order for our bodies to start working again we have to begin to take food. As we do this, our digestive system comes back into action, and with it a hunger for food.

The spiritual is like the natural. While we have fellowship with the Lord in prayer and reading His Word, we are continually being filled. The spiritual hunger and thirst is normal and active, as is a natural hunger and thirst in a healthy body.

If we stop eating and drinking spiritually — to read an ordinary book instead of God's Word, to talk to a friend about our problems instead of talking to the Lord, to slip back into living completely in the sense realm, ignoring the spiritual life — it seems that our desire for the spiritual food goes to sleep in the same way that the natural digestive system goes to sleep when it is not stimulated.

Just as an effort is required to break a natural fast by beginning to take food, so it is in the spiritual realm. We have to create an appetite by seeking the Lord and reading His Word. Usually there are no feelings to help us and no sense of excitement, because our spiritual tastebuds have gone to sleep. We do not have the first thrill of meeting the Lord, like we had when we were born again and became Christians; our renewed hunger and thirst for the Lord is by our choice and simple determination to seek His face and to hear from Him.

One day the Lord gave me a special vision when I was praying. I saw myself lowering a large bucket into an old-fashioned well, bringing it up brimful of water. I unhooked the bucket and stood it on the ground, and then I saw many people of different nationalities standing round the well with cups in their hands. One by one I took their cups and gave them water from my bucket until it was empty.

Then the Lord said to me, "Let down the bucket again."

I did so and brought it up full, thinking I would be repeating my previous action by giving those people water to drink, but the Lord said to me, "I want *you* to drink that bucketful."

I was so surprised, and exclaimed, "How can I drink a bucketful of water?", for I knew that to drink one glassful of water was about the limit of my capacity.

The Lord answered, "Your capacity for drinking spiritually is far greater than your natural drinking capacity."

I took up the bucketful of water and began to drink. I did not stop — I drank and I drank and I drank, until I had emptied the bucket. Then the Lord said, "Let down your bucket again."

I obeyed, and wondered if He was going to tell me that I had to drink the second bucketful. After I had placed it on the ground, the Lord said, "I want you to look into the bucket and use it as a mirror."

I bent over and peered into the surface of the water. The Lord asked, "Who do you see?"

My reply was immediate and without thought, for I answered "Jesus."

I could hardly believe the word that had come from my mouth, or the revelation that was conveyed through that vision. If I drink deeply enough and long enough — in other words, if I will seek Him and will pursue what He shows me — then I will discover my spiritual capacity for drinking. Not only will others see Jesus in me, but I too will see Jesus in me. I will know complete oneness with Him. He who lives within me will be as a well of living water, and I shall never thirst again.

I will know a walk with Him where my step will be sure and steadfast, my joy full and my cup running over.

11

Insight

As we seek the Lord, He brings to the surface things needing to be dealt with in our lives — even things of which we are not conscious. I remember on one occasion when praying in tongues the Lord gave me as a vision a close-up picture of an Arab's head and shoulders, so clear that I could almost describe the features. As I continued praying, the vision changed and I saw a street scene with many Arabs — men, women and children. It was almost as if I was aware of the smells in the market place and could hear the noise of their chatter.

I started to weep, not knowing why I was weeping. I began to feel such a love for those people, and the words that came from my lips were "Can the Arabs be saved too?"

The Lord answered, "Whosoever."

I had grown up overhearing conversations about

the confrontation which existed between the Arabs and the Jews, and, because the Jews are God's chosen people, I had concluded that the Arabs could not be saved. They were filed away somewhere deep in my subconscious as being a race of people that God did not love, otherwise I would never have asked Him if the Arabs could be saved.

What divine miracles are wrought within us when we seek God's face, for the prejudice which had been buried deep within me — even without my giving it any direct thought — had not been in line with God's thinking and God's love. Jesus came to save the world, and no matter what enmity might exist between people and nations, the love and sacrifice made on Calvary for our salvation was for all who will believe on the Lord Jesus Christ, because all who call upon Him shall be saved, according to God's Word. His love knows no bounds, but any limits in my thinking or subconscious mind had to be broken.

I had another longer and much more painful experience, when I found it difficult to understand another member of the Body of Christ. Not only was I confronted with the barriers in that person, but I also set up barriers because often I was unwilling to accept help offered from that person. As a result, I did not give the fellowship and trust that was needed to set the other person free.

The Lord continued to deal with my own heart and my old way of thinking, and gradually brought me into a new and enlarged place in Him where it did not matter whether or not the other person changed. I was changed by being taken into a new depth of God's love and a willingness to receive His help through a channel of His choice.

Looking back, I realise that I could have read a number of books on how to relate to others — in fact I could have gained much knowledge of why the other person and myself reacted in the way that we did — but through prayer and wanting to be right before God, He did a work in me that could never have been achieved through knowledge given by a book.

Sometimes the Lord in His wisdom keeps hidden from us things that we could not bear without being affected in the wrong way. I remember seeking the Lord over a certain matter time and time again, and all He would say to me was "Trust me." I could not understand why He did not give me some insight as to why certain things were happening, but in His wisdom He had to keep hidden those things that would have affected me, making me frustrated or bitter because of the events.

I thank Him for being the all-seeing Father, protecting me from information that I could not handle and covering others involved until I had grown to a place in Him where He could reveal details to me and in His love I could remain unaffected.

I have observed changes taking place in the lives of others. One married couple seemed to have insurmountable barriers between them, in spite of the fact that they loved each other and loved the Lord. The barriers, which seemed indefinable, took them round and round in an endless circle of events, keeping them captive in lack of understanding and right communication, resulting in much frustration.

Both husband and wife continued to seek the Lord, not just over weeks, or even months, but over a number of years. They came to a new place of praying in tongues daily, and the Lord was able to touch them both. Without my knowing the details of what He has been able to bring to the surface and bring out, I see the evidence of oneness and partnership, yes, even a new love lighting their eyes for each other and for the Lord.

While praying in tongues with another person, I began to feel that I was battling against something. I did not know what was happening, but just abandoned myself to expressing loudly in tongues the stirring I felt and which I could not understand.

Suddenly this person stopped praying in tongues. I knew that I had to go on, but I did not feel free to continue praying in her presence under the influence of what I was feeling.

I stood up and said, "I must continue praying. I will go for a walk to be alone with the Lord."

There was a resistance within me to her silence and I had no idea that she had stopped praying in tongues because she could not bear what was coming through me. I did not know what I was feeling but I knew I had to get out of that room and get alone with the Lord so I could pour out in tongues and let the Holy Spirit make the necessary intercession through me.

I walked for an hour in the rain along a deserted beach, praying out loud in tongues and letting the utterances pour forth without any restriction. I felt an urgency, and I could not stop praying until something changed within me — almost as if the sea had been calmed or a battle won, or a mission accomplished.

A peace descended upon me and I later discovered that a peace had come upon my friend at the same time. Two or three days later she shared with me how the Lord had dealt with her. In the past she had had many battles concerning criticism and had tried to break the habit which had plagued her for so long, but now the Lord had revealed to her that it was a critical spirit which needed to be dealt with and removed. This victory had been won because of our praying together and my continued intercession along the beach that morning.

If only the people of God would seek His face and allow Him to remove what needs to be removed, to replace right thinking for wrong thinking — because He can arrange the right circumstances, yes, the right ministry too, that will bring us out of our bondages and afflictions into His wholeness.

12

The Leader's Wisdom

We are called to walk by faith and not by sight, and discovering how to pray in one situation does not give us a formula on how to pray in another similar situation. I discovered this when praying about my own physical body.

In 1970, and while nursing my invalid husband, my body began to feel the effects due to the strain placed upon me at that time. My heart had begun to pound, and fatigue and exhaustion seemed to be knocking at my door. For the first time in my life I was facing physical weakness.

My workload was tremendously eased at that time, as I had the help of two young American women — one to do the housework and one to help me look after my husband — so I made a decision to fast concerning all that was happening in my life and particularly in my body. I not only went into a fast, I began to sleep, only rousing myself to do the tasks that I personally needed to do, and leaving most of the work to be done by my helpers.

I felt guilty because I was not praying as well as fasting, as I thought this should be the procedure. I fasted and slept, having only water to drink for two whole weeks, and the miracle performed in my body was beyond my wildest dreams. I was renewed spiritually, physically and mentally; in fact I felt like a new woman, full of vitality and strength, and was disappointed when the Lord spoke to me and told me to break my fast. I had wanted to continue, as I was beginning to enjoy my fellowship with Him in new ways, as well as the healing of my body. I gave Him my thanks for healing me and making my heart behave normally.

Two years later my heart started troubling me again, pounding incessantly, making me conscious of its activity all through the day and giving me intermittent sleep at night. I could only lie on my back, for to turn on either side meant increased pounding of my heart, and even on my back I had to have extra pillows to help ease my condition.

I told the Lord that the challenge was not going to affect me. He had healed me two thousand years ago when He died on the cross, and I believed His Word that He bore my sicknesses and my infirmities and by His stripes I was healed. The manifestation of the healing had come to my body two years previously and I was going to remain unaffected by the lie which was challenging me again.

However, this did not bring healing or stop my heart from pounding, and as the weeks went by the strain became apparent on my face, for my friend questioned me concerning my physical condition. When I shared with her what was happening, she was not only concerned but said it was vital that I had proper sleep because of all that was required of me during my waking hours.

I told her in no uncertain terms that I was not going to ask the Lord to heal me again, for He had healed me and I would continue to ignore the lie that was in my body. She insisted that I could not carry on without sufficient sleep, and so I replied, "All right, I will ask the Lord to give me sleep, but I am not going to ask Him to heal me because He has healed me." I knew that I had not asked Him to give me sleep before, and I also knew that in His Word it says that "He gives his beloved sleep." I talked to the Lord about it, asking Him to give me sleep and thanking Him for doing so.

However, He did not answer that prayer! While I could not understand His apparent ignoring of my request, I did not get fussed about it. I did not go into panic or fear, neither did I think I was out with the Lord because He had not granted my request, or imagine that I might have committed some sin or grieved Him in some way without my knowing it. In fact, I said to Him, "I do not understand why You have not given me sleep, Lord. I have asked You, and I know You are able to do this for me, for Your power is great and knows no bounds."

So I determined I would use my sleepless hours. I

would praise Him and I would pray — although I must admit that my enthusiasm for prayer was not at a height where I would rather pray than sleep!

This went on for a while, until one night I was so exasperated with the condition of my heart and the way it kept me awake that I sat upright in bed. I did not ask God to do anything, in fact I was not talking to Him about the matter at all. With a finger pointed, I spoke out loud and said, "Heart, in the name of Jesus I command you to function properly and to behave yourself."

Once those words had come out of my mouth, and I had heard them, I knew the matter was dealt with. I had discovered the reason why the Lord had not answered my prayer and given me sleep. He was waiting for me to take command in the situation and to speak, by the power of His Holy Spirit, life-giving words to my own heart.

I threw away the extra pillows immediately, slid down the bed and went immediately into a peaceful sleep. I was never disturbed again through the pounding of my heart until, seven years later, I was faced with the challenge yet once again.

I was in Sweden staying in the home of a Christian family, and had been enjoying some long walks through the snow-covered woods and fields, when suddenly the trouble with my heart began again.

I ignored it, hoping it would go away, but it only grew worse to the point that it was alarming. The pounding was so severe that it was frightening. I remembered the word of authority that I had given to my heart and how it had obeyed. I decided it must continue to obey the word of authority, and so again I repeated what I had done seven years earlier. I commanded my heart in the name of the Lord Jesus to function properly — to cease from its pounding, and for everything that was out of order to come into order.

Nothing changed, and my word appeared to have no authority or backing. It was like an instruction falling upon deaf ears, and I was almost ready to panic that it had not worked as before.

I talked to the Lord and I thanked Him for His health that He gave up on Calvary — yes, for all the benefits that I received from His life laid down — His righteousness for my unrighteousness, His separation from Father because of my sin, that I might come into the presence of Father and no longer be separated.

I thought over the perfect exchange that had taken place on the Cross. I also thanked Him that in His presence there was fulness of joy and that He had given His peace to me. I felt I was in a struggle to remain in that peace, for daily I was becoming more and more frightened, because the pounding was so great that I had become sore on my left side and I knew by my clothing that there must be some swelling in evidence.

My thoughts were so negative, and I wondered if I was going to have a heart attack or a stroke, or maybe I would suddenly die. I tried to push these negative thoughts and fears away from me. It was a help during the day to be amongst people, but the biggest trial was when I was on my own in my room at night. I propped myself up in bed to ease my condition, realising that while I was trying to appear normal during the day I was succumbing to an invalid state at night.

I discovered that pushing fears away does not deal with them, and in the middle of one night I told the Lord that I must deal with this matter before Him. I said, "Lord, I have three fears that are troubling me, and I am going to look those three fears straight in the eye before You. I am going to acknowledge that I have them in order that I might get free from them. Here they are, Lord, I name them one by one."

I pointed to three fingers, and I said, "One, I am afraid that I might have a heart attack. Two, I am afraid I might have a stroke, and three, I am frightened that I might drop down dead." I added that I did not think I was frightened of going to be with the Lord, but I was frightened of this happening in a foreign country and while I was a visitor in someone else's home.

As I spoke out loud I continued, "Here they are, Lord, my three fears," and I held up three fingers to the Lord. Then I said, "Can I trust You, Lord, not to let any one of those three things happen to me?"

I shall never forget my experience, for immediately a peace came to my mind; in fact the whole room seemed to be filled with a peace that made me look round as if I might "see" peace. For, while my room had been absolutely silent apart from my voice speaking to the Lord, now it was pervaded with the Prince of Peace.

My fears left me, even though my heart continued to pound. For days I could not think a negative thought about anything, almost as if my mind had been purged and cleansed.

I had once again been delivered. From my fears? Yes, and from my physical disability, even though it took just over a year for my heart to come into line with my bclicving.

I learnt so much through these challenges; certainly that there is no fixed pattern for prayer, that there are keys to find in the various challenges that we have, and that the Lord does not withhold Himself without a good reason. I also learnt how important it is to bring every thought into captivity to Christ (2 Cor. 10:5). We must face the fears that would cripple and bring them captive to the Prince of Peace who keeps our hearts and minds in the love of God, free from all fear.

He brings us to a place where we trust Him more and more by the way that He helps us and answers our prayers. But then He begins to trust us and our confidence in Him, in order that He might bring us into maturity and into a place where He can reveal insight into the Kingdom of God — insight that shows our position in Him, new depths of our inheritance, and a wakening reality that He has conquered death and that His resurrection life in us is the victory over Satan and the powers of darkness.

13

Directions

It has been my delight to discover that the Lord is interested in the simple details which make up my life. I have discovered this by the way He has answered some of my prayers; and I have been encouraged to have confidence in talking to Him about anything, realising that nothing is too small or too big for His interest.

I casually said to the Lord one day, "I never hear anything about what You are doing in France; it is so near to England, and yet so remote that it could be the other side of the world. Is there anything happening in France, Lord? If there is, I would love to hear about it."

A short time after this, during an Easter holiday, a stranger telephoned me saying that she was a missionary working in the south of France, and had been given my name and address by a friend of hers whom I had met when I was in the United States.

She said that she would be passing through Ipswich with an English missionary and a young French woman and could they call and meet me.

How quickly the Lord had answered my prayer, giving me a little first hand information concerning some of the things that He was doing in France. Those missionaries came from a university area, where many students were giving their lives to the Lord and were being filled with the Holy Spirit. They shared a few details of what was happening in other areas, and for a bonus I was given an invitation to stay in their home should I ever be passing through France.

Not only have I discovered that the Lord is interested and answers my prayers concerning seemingly insignificant things, but I have discovered the simplicity of His guidance. In fact it almost seems so natural that I have to learn to recognise His leading and those little nudges that I could so easily miss.

There was one occasion when I felt I should visit a lady who lived on the other side of the town. On arrival I discovered that I had not called at a convenient time, and could only stay a few minutes before starting my return journey home.

I was telling the Lord that it seemed a fruitless journey, and could not understand why I had felt I should make that visit. As I was driving home, the woman's sister came to my mind and I felt an urge to visit her. I did not know her very well and had never been to her home; for a minute or two I was tempted to think it was my own idea and that I was trying to justify my outing that evening. However, I decided to follow my thoughts through, and on my arrival I was invited in with a look of shocked surprise.

The woman said very little and I found myself not only talking about the Lord, but sharing different parts of my testimony with a flow that did not have to be aided by any questions or seeking on her part, neither was my conversation hindered by her silence.

Some weeks later she was able to share with me that she had planned to commit suicide that night. My visit, and what I had shared, had intercepted her plans and had reversed the situation.

One day I needed to telephone the United States to deliver a message to a friend but was surprised to discover that I had mistakenly dialed the number of my friend's mother. I apologised but, before replacing the receiver, I enquired how she was and discovered that she was a sick woman. I immediately said, "I have not dialed the wrong number, the Lord caused me to do this."

"Will you pray for me?" she asked.

I prayed, first of all thanking the Lord for directing my telephone call and then asking Him to heal and fully restore her.

Her faith was stimulated by my telephone call,

which at first appeared to be a mistake but which we both realised was the Lord's guidance. She responded to my prayer and received her healing and testified to what God had done. I marvelled at the natural leading of the Lord and how He could cause someone to call from England because He was wanting to deliver a woman in America from her affliction.

A fisherman I know, who was on the Isle of Skye, suddenly felt one day that he should pray, and so he retreated to his caravan home and spent a time praying in tongues — not knowing why he should be praying, for the Lord had not given him any enlightenment.

Later that day, his two sons returned to harbour with his damaged fishing boat. The boat had been holed when they hit a rock and had turned on its side. If another strong wave had hit it, the boat would probably have broken into pieces and his sons would have been lost.

When the father enquired of the sons at what time they were in trouble, he realised that it was when he was on his knees in prayer. God protected and brought his sons and boat back to safety. How thankful he was that he had obeyed the leading of the Holy Spirit.

Some months later that fisherman's wife was due to have an operation which would last for three hours. He could not be in their home town and had to remain on the Isle of Skye due to his work. However, he determined that he would start praying at nine o'clock in the morning, the time appointed for the operation, and continue for the three hours in order to cover his wife in prayer while she was in the operating theatre.

At about ten-fifteen he began to feel hungry because he had had no breakfast, and thought that he would quickly stop and have something to eat but the Lord revealed to him that he should go on praying. He continued until eleven-thirty, when He knew from the Lord that he could stop praying and that the operation was completed and successful, even though he had been told that it would be a three-hour operation. Later it was confirmed to him that the operation had finished at that time.

We should not wonder if we find ourselves doing things we had not planned to do, or find ourselves in certain places at certain times, for this is part of our natural walk with the Lord.

One morning, for some unknown reason, I asked the Lord whether I should do my shopping in the morning or in the afternoon. He said, "In the afternoon."

I do not normally ask Him when I should go shopping; it is something that I usually fit in amongst my other commitments. However, that day I set out for the town after lunch and had only gone a short distance from my house when I met a young man, whom at first I did not recognise — the last time I had seen him he was a little boy. When I recognised him I would have stopped, but he hastened on. I then remembered that I had heard that he had made a mess of his life and would have nothing to do with God. My one mile walk into town was a walk of prayer for that young man, and from then onwards I continued to be led in prayer on his behalf.

It could be that there is no-one else in the world praying for that young man, and the Lord had to find a way to bring him to the attention of a member of the Body of Christ in order that intercession might be made for him.

I am so thankful that I have been discovering the delights of having fellowship with the Lord and the wisdom in letting the Holy Spirit lead me concerning matters for which I am to pray. If I take on too much in prayer, because I know prayer is needed, I become like an overloaded power line that breaks down under the strain.

I used to feel gloomy when I thought of all the people in need and the many missionaries and organisations and enterprises needing prayer. I felt swamped before I even got started and wanted to bury my head in the sand like an ostrich so I could not see or hear what was going on around me.

The task that appears to be endless and insurmountable brings forth a reaction to deal with the pressure. While the pressure can take some into successful action, it can cause many of us to ignore the matter altogether and do nothing; or it can cause us to strive so hard to attain to the standard which we think we should have that we lose the joy and thrill of the ministry of prayer.

The Holy Spirit helps us and the more fruit we see from our praying the more we are encouraged to pray. He enables us to use our faith, showing us how to be free from fears and doubts, causing us to enter in to the ministry of praying — a ministry guided and anointed by the Holy Spirit.

It is interesting to observe the way that prayer is channelled and how members of the Body of Christ receive instructions from the Lord concerning their particular targets in prayer.

One young woman shared with me how the Lord had directed her to a flat which is on a hill overlooking the city for which she had been burdened to pray. Her excitement had grown and was clearly expressed as she shared the details of the way the Lord had provided the flat for her, and how she enjoyed that hidden ministry of prayer. On one occasion the Lord had told her to "compass the city" and pray in tongues; she had obeyed and walked round the outside of her city praying. The interesting fact that emerged was that two or three days after she had done this the police found a murderer for whom they had been seeking for many, many weeks and whom they had not been able to find.

From other details that she has shared, I can see that she is alert to news concerning what is happening in that city and is growing in discernment as to what to pray and when to pray, and how to observe the events that are going on round about her.

I know another person who has been directed by the Lord to pray for pregnant mothers, and it seems to work out that He gives her about six to pray for at a time. She is in prayer for them during their nine months of pregnancy, covering the mother and the unborn child.

One thirty-seven-year-old mother, who had had many problems and several miscarriages was on her list. The nine months pregnancy and labour were normal, and the baby completely normal too. Another was having a difficult pregnancy and there were fears that the baby might be lost or born abnormal, but, I believe through this prayer ministry, a normal baby was brought into the world.

I know a young widow to whom the Lord has given the ministry of praying for unmarried girls who are frustrated and disappointed, or anxious and worried about the fact that they are unmarried. The Lord brings to her attention those for whom she is to pray.

I know of one who was led to take on in prayer a baby boy where the family circumstances were such that it was vital that prayer should be made for the child. I can testify to the faithfulness of the prayer ministry concerning this boy, for often the heartaches and prayers have been poured out in my presence. I have watched this ministry over a number of years, and have observed the moving of God in the circumstances of this boy, with the result of his coming to know the Lord Jesus as Saviour and committing his life fully to the Lord.

I get so excited when I see the way the Lord can direct each one of His people in prayer, giving us specific goals for which to aim. It does not necessarily mean that we have only one goal or that we do not pray about anything else, but at least we are set free from being put off or crippled by the magnitude of the prayer ministry.

While individuals can be given specific objectives by the Lord, so also can whole fellowships be given united ministry in this way. My own fellowship was directed a number of years ago to pray for the Spanish-speaking people. This was remarkable in itself, because not one of us was particularly drawn to the Spanish people more than any other nationality and not one of us could speak Spanish, but the result has been so rewarding and dynamic. We not only made contact with a Spanish translator but we have been able to send thousands of books in Spanish to South America and Spain. The fellowship not only prayed but also gave of their money to pay for these books, and by the time we began to receive letters in Spanish one member of our fellowship — directed by the Lord — had learnt and become fluent in reading and writing the Spanish language.

Our directed, concentrated praying can be like laser beams upon countries and nations. It can be like an arrow sent forth, aimed and directed on target by the Holy Spirit in the lives of individuals.

14

Inspired by Vision

I have discovered that the simplicity of the Lord's guidance through visions has helped my faith and my praying and has led me into a dimension of prayer which I could not have reached without them.

One evening in a meeting we were checking a certain matter with the Lord, and He gave a vision to one member of the group of a train being held up at a level crossing, waiting for all the road traffic to pass through. This was completely opposite to what normally happens, for it is always the traffic on the road which has to wait until the train has passed.

By this simple vision the Lord was showing us that what we thought was the obvious course to our way of thinking was not His way in that particular situation.

On one occasion I was asked to pray for an

elderly man who seemed to have a number of things wrong with him, including high blood pressure and depression. In no way could I have prayed in faith and received his healing, so I used my gift of praying in tongues.

As I prayed the Lord gave me a vision of an old violin with its bridge and strings broken. The bow strings were broken too, and as I looked at the vision I saw a pair of hands begin to clean and polish the instrument. The strings were set in place and the bow re-strung. The same pair of hands then took the violin and began to play it. Through that vision I was able to believe and could then pray with my understanding. I asked the Lord to restore and heal the man and to take that aged 'instrument' and make him useful for His glory.

On another occasion I had been staying in the home of a man who had collected antiques over a number of years, and in his kitchen stood an old copper kettle no longer in use.

One morning I found the owner cleaning that old kettle and I watched him as he rubbed the cloth over the surface and noticed a number of small dents that remained dull and unpolished. I asked him if he ever used a brush or tried to polish it to remove the darkness and dull appearance in the dents where the polishing cloth did not reach.

"Oh, no," he replied, "it would lose some of its beauty, which lies in its aged appearance." He was not trying to make it look like new; he wanted the old copper kettle to be seen for its beauty and the usefulness it once had.

Two weeks after this incident, I was praying for a church that had had a difficult time and was without a pastor. The Lord gave me in a vision the scene in that kitchen with the old copper kettle being polished and appreciated. I waited on the Lord so that He could make clear to me what He was saying through that vision in connection with the church.

He showed me that all that the church had stood for in the past, its work and its activities had been good; but He was now wanting them to lay aside the old because He had a new method of operation for them — something that was fitting for this day and age. The old was not to be thrown out and despised or cast away — it could be looked upon and admired and retained with the memories of service well done. He wanted their attention to be drawn to what He desired for them at this present time. Just as my host had a modern whistling kettle in use, I could see that the Lord had something new to give to that church which would be suitable for what He is doing today.

I was able to share the vision with the fellowship and give the encouragement that they needed. I knew that if they sought the Lord He would make plain His purpose for them. They were not to be so set in their old ways as to make it impossible for them to receive the new.

A teacher working in a Junior school was able to run a Christian club in the lunch hour. She asked me to pray for eleven children who had given their lives to Jesus as a result of the club. Most of the children did not have Christian parents and backgrounds to help them and, as far as was known, there would be no further help given to them at the senior schools to which they would be going.

She was concerned for them, and felt that in their baby stage as Christians they would not be able to grow without help.

My mind could so easily have told me that it would be very hard for those children to develop in the Lord without encouragement and Bible study, and without being amongst other Christians — plus the fact that they would be surrounded by other children who could lead them astray and along so many of the paths of the enemy. I said to the Lord, "What shall I pray? What can I believe for these children?"

Immediately to my mind's eye came a bag of dried peas and I pondered on the vision which the Lord had given to me. Dried peas are preserved peas, and they can be kept for a long time, but when soaked in water and cooked they become full of flavour and nourishment.

I then knew what to pray, and it was not hard to believe for those children to be preserved from rotting away, as peas would rot if not preserved. I could believe for their protection against evil and their coming forth at the right time to be soaked in the life of the Lord and to be fruitful in His kingdom.

My faith had needed help and stimulation for me to believe, and the Lord used the simple illustration of the dried peas in order that I might pray a definite prayer of protection and preservation for those young folk — a prayer for growth to come forth at the right time, and ministries to flow through them at some future date.

15

Team-work Inaugurated

One of the blessings of using the gift of tongues in prayer is that we can continue praying for a person or a situation long after we have run out of English words. If I use my own native language in which to pray, then I am praying with my understanding, but to please God it must be in faith. It is one thing to pour out all the details of a need or a request, and it is another thing to be in faith to receive the answer.

It is easier to believe when my mind is not in the way, so by praying in tongues I can continue for a much longer period of time than when praying in English. The Holy Spirit within makes intercession before God on behalf of the person or situation which is on my heart, and for which I desire His help and intervention.

I have discovered this gift to be a weapon against the enemy: it is a mystery and I cannot comprehend with my natural mind how it works. All I know is that when I have used the gift, powers of darkness have been dealt with. I have also discovered that group praying in this way is mighty; in fact the Lord Himself has so encouraged me to believe this by the way He has led and the results I have witnessed.

One of my earliest experiences of praying with a group all speaking in tongues together was in 1970, when we arranged a barbecue as an outreach for young people in the Ipswich area. It was the very first time we had joined to intercede in tongues together, and during that time the Lord gave me a vision of a figure like the Olympic runner, carrying a flaming torch and running not only over the field where the barbecue was to be held but also through the streets of Ipswich. I knew that this runner depicted the Holy Spirit, and sensed that if I stopped praying the runner would stop running.

Excitement welled up within me, as well as a sense of urgency and purpose, because of my desire to see the runner proceed throughout the whole town. I had never had such a vision before, but I believed that I was working in oneness with the Holy Spirit and that something was being done concerning the young people in Ipswich and the barbecue that we had arranged.

A few of us went into the town and handed out invitations to the young people on the streets, believing that the Holy Spirit would draw out many from all over the town for this event. For those who had no means of transport, we felt directed of the Lord to hire two coaches to take them to the field which had been loaned to us by a Christian farmer for this outreach. We had no idea what was in store for us, but we saw the power of the Holy Spirit controlling the whole event.

Eighty skinheads had decided to occupy the buses that we had provided, and it was obvious from the outset that they were intent on doing all they could to ruin the occasion. We had booked a Christian music group and a minister to speak in between the musical items, and those skinheads plus others created so much noise and disturbance in front of the platform that it was very hard for both the group and the minister.

Fortunately the loudspeaker system was good and reached the perimeter of the field where many had retreated. At one point the leader of the group sought me out and asked me to rally my workers to mingle with the troublemakers in front of the platform, for many of them had made a journey to the nearest village public house and the drinking had only increased their rowdiness and activities.

We had a large bonfire to help create a barbecue atmosphere, as well as smaller fires to cook the food. The troublemakers had begun to throw their lighted cigarette ends in any direction, and the stage and the seating facilities in that field consisted of bales of straw. The scene was fraught with danger and I made my way round to the back of the stage and prayed.

I knew I had no workers to draw on to come and help, because they were all busy cooking and serving food. As I prayed, the Lord reminded me of the vision of the Olympic runner, for I had seen him running over that whole field. I could then pray in faith and believe that the whole field and everyone in it would be completely protected that night.

I placed myself quite near to the platform, where I could keep a closer eye on everything that was happening. The minister announced that he was going to ask a lady to go to the platform to share her testimony and I was alarmingly surprised when he announced me as the person!

I made my way to the platform, having no idea what I would say. I stood before the microphone amidst boos and rowdy shouting. The leader of the musical group came to the microphone and asked them to give me a chance, but his plea was unheard. He did not want me to stand on my own before that microphone but I assured him that I was quite all right. I waited silently and, as I waited, the Holy Spirit began to work, and gradually a hush came upon that field until there was complete silence.

I started to speak, and stated that in my younger days I had not given much thought to God and I had had no desire to find out about Him. My mother and brothers were Christians, but because there were so many religions I had wondered how they could know that theirs was the right one. They said that God heard and answered prayer, but because I could not see or hear Him I did not know whether or not to believe that He existed.

I continued, and said that at the age of

twenty-nine, happily married and with two small children, I felt that I could no longer shelve this issue. I decided that I really had to find out if there was a God who loved and cared and answered prayer in the way that I had heard many people relate throughout the years. In my search I spoke out loud in my own home, saying, "God, if You are there, if You exist, if You can hear me talking to You now, I want to know. If there is a right road and a wrong road, I want to be on the right road. If there is a heaven and a hell, I want to go to heaven, but I do not know. If You can hear me, will You help me?"

I had thought to myself that if God did exist He must be greater than anything or anyone and He must answer that request. I could not make a decision on anyone else's testimony or convictions; I had *got* to know for myself.

God took many steps to answer that prayer, and I discovered for myself that He is real. I continued by telling them how months later I had knelt down in my own home and asked God to come into my life. I told Him that I did not see Jesus die on the cross or rise from the tomb but, because the Bible says that He died and rose again and that He did it for me, I was going to believe Him, and I asked Him to take me and make me His child. From that time on my life was different. My thinking and my habits changed and I really did have a new life; I proved that God heard and answered prayer.

I ended my talk by saying that if anyone wanted to know God, they too could prove that He existed.

I left the platform and the music group began to play, but one young skinhead sought me out and said, "I liked what you had to say, but I am an atheist, although I did pray once."

I asked him what he had prayed and he said, "Well, it was like this: I had to go before the court for a serious offence and there were other offences to be taken into account, and I asked God to get me off."

I enquired, "What happened?"

"Well, I don't really know, but it was serious and there were the other cases that they were considering, but the judge let me off."

Immediately I replied, "So the Lord answered your prayer."

"Well," he said, "if He would just answer once more and let me win the football pools, I'll believe!"

I learnt something more about our wonderful God through this encounter. He leaves no stone unturned to reveal Himself and to answer every cry that is made to Him, even to those like that young man, who only called upon God for help when he was in a tight corner. God, in His love and mercy, wanted him to know that He had heard him and wanted to help and save him.

While there is no evidence to show that any gave

their lives to the Lord through that barbecue, the benefits of what we found through praying for that outreach are continuous.

Most times when I am praying for Ipswich, the Lord reminds me of the vision of the Olympic runner and also of His word in Ephesians 3:20 — **"He is able to do exceeding abundantly above all that we ask or think, according to the power that worketh in us."** Various changes and Christian growth have taken place in Ipswich, crusades have been held and many souls saved. Only the Lord knows how much He has been able to do through the intercession of His people in Ipswich. Some of the things were beyond my thinking and consequently beyond my asking; but even if I could have thought of them, they would have been beyond the reach of my faith.

Because of God's word, I now dare to believe that while our minds were centred on the barbecue, the Holy Spirit — the power within us — made intercession as we prayed in tongues on behalf of Ipswich which was far beyond the barbecue. The answer to that prayer is still being fulfilled.

16

Working as a Team

Another step of growth for our fellowship took place when the baby of one of our families became ill; every time he cut a tooth he had bronchitis. Antibiotics had been administered by the doctor, relieving this condition as each tooth was cut.

On one particular occasion he was cutting another tooth and once again developed the chest infection. While the parents were praying the Lord spoke to them and asked them to trust Him without going to the doctor. Speaking to the mother on the telephone one morning, she said the condition was getting worse, but they had gone back to the Lord in prayer and still felt that they were doing what He required of them.

After about two more days the mother telephoned again, and said, "Freda, will you please seek the Lord, for there is no improvement — in fact it has been so hard watching him deteriorate when we know that the medicine from the doctor has always given relief. We want to go through with the Lord, but will you please check that we are hearing right."

We knew that the condition of the baby was serious because a nurse in our fellowship who had visited the home remarked that she was convinced that he had pneumonia.

After the telephone call three of us went into prayer. The Lord gave one a scripture and another a vision, and both indicated that He was in control and that the parents had heard aright. The Lord spoke to me and said, "Ask the fellowship to fast and pray this day for the baby."

I went into action to contact as many members as possible. This was a new venture for us as we had never fasted as a group. It was a little difficult for those at work to pray, but they were willing to give their lunch hours interceding on behalf of the baby.

I visited the home about four o'clock that afternoon and was taken to the child's bedroom. He opened his eyes and smiled at his mother — the first smile he had given for days. It was the turning point, and over the days that followed he gradually improved and came right through without any medical help. The miracle continued, because he cut the remainder of his teeth without having bronchitis again.

The Lord was opening our eyes to what can be achieved when a group will join in prayer and seek

His face. That family went through the trauma of the experience so that God could cause us to see what can be achieved through united prayer.

On reflection I can see how from time to time the Lord continued to show us the value of a group praying in tongues together.

A few years back, when the firemen were due to go on strike in this country, we felt that we should pray the night before the strike was due to begin. As we sought the Lord we were guided as to what we could believe.

We prayed and declared that there would be no loss of life or injury in Ipswich due to the firemen being on strike. To the best of my knowledge, this was so.

On another occasion, when my younger daughter was in New Zealand, I had felt very burdened one day on her behalf. I prayed on my own for her, but did not feel relieved of the heaviness that was upon me.

I tried to contact her by telephone, only to discover that she had moved from one place to another area, and I had no way of knowing her whereabouts.

As we gathered for prayer that evening I shared with the fellowship the burden that I had carried all day and asked them to join me in prayer for her.

At that time we had a young woman in our group

who, I think mainly due to shyness, could not bring herself to pray in tongues aloud with the rest of us, and so whenever we did this she would always go to another room on her own, rejoining us after we had finished. She did not seem to be bothered about this and, because of the way she handled it, the rest of us felt at liberty to pray even though she could not remain in the room.

I saw her leave the room as we started to pray and knew that she would be happy on her own while we were interceding together. I was unaware that after a brief period she had re-entered the room and joined us.

I became disturbed at the vision the Lord gave to me while we were in prayer. I saw a large octupus in the sea, wrapping its tentacles round my daughter. My praying became intense, and in my vision I saw myself jumping into the water and getting hold of a tentacle to pull it away from her, but as fast as I pulled one away another would entwine her.

I had a feeling of fear as we prayed, and knew that I was calling upon the Lord for help. Again my vision changed and I saw the rest of the group jumping into the water, each of them taking one tentacle, and as the group did this together she was released.

The scene changed and I saw us on a grassy bank, panting for breath, and my daughter lying exhausted but safe. I had felt the tension as we prayed, and knew that only a limited time would be available in the natural to a person being trapped under water. Once I had seen the rescue operation complete I knew that our praying was complete too.

I was surprised when I opened my eyes to find that the young woman had re-entered the room to join us for prayer. After I had shared my vision, she said to me, "An octupus has eight tentacles and there are eight of us in this room"

I knew the Lord was doing more than one thing through us that night. Apart from anything He had done for my daughter, He was also showing the young woman that she played a vital part in the praying group. Her presence, and the operation of the Holy Spirit through her, was vital too.

Another victory was won through the group praying in tongues together when I discovered that a neighbour of mine, living the opposite side of the main road, was ill. The news was given to me through her married daughter, who stated that her mother was on the verge of a breakdown; she was in deep depression and could no longer leave the house.

It was obvious that the daughter was worried, and I told her that the next time the group met in my home to pray we would seek God on behalf of her mother. Her tears began to flow as she thanked me and hastily drove off in her car.

There were a dozen or more at the next meeting and we joined together in praying for my neighbour, who was unknown to the rest of the group.

It seemed that we had a united determination, which had been given to us by the Holy Spirit, so that we could not stop praying until we knew that something had been done for her. The Lord by His Spirit brought us into unity of faith and we realised that we were going against the enemy and that we had authority over him. We pronounced the woman loosed from the powers of darkness, from the spirit of fear, and from all the effects that the depression was having on her and her family.

We knew that we had the victory and had declared the word of authority which had to be obeyed.

The next day I wondered whether or not I should visit her and tell her that we had prayed, but as I was not sure what to do, I did not do anything.

A few days later I was tidying the front garden, when I saw my neighbour and her daughter emerge from their house. I called out with the question "How are you?"

The daughter immediately shouted back, "One hundred per cent better."

I crossed the busy road to go to them, and the daughter's words were "I said that if this worked, I would believe." Again the tears came to her eyes, and before I could reply she had climbed into her car and driven off, leaving me standing on the pavement with her mother.

The woman looked so well and alive, and not at all depressed. She said, "Mrs Flude, you ***will*** thank your group for praying for me. I was in such a bad way, I had terrible thoughts which I could not get rid of, and I was unable to sleep. But one night I thought to myself, those people are praying for me and I needn't be like this any longer." She went on to say that it was just as if something left her and she was set free. In fact she said that she had already booked a holiday.

How I rejoiced and thanked God, not only for this avenue of prayer and outreach to my neighbour, but I thanked Him that there was a group of us learning to intercede and to go against the strongholds of Satan.

We have known times of praying together in this way when it has been so hard to pray, and not one of us would have continued if we had been on our own. We have only been able to carry on in determination, making ourselves speak in tongues, because we have been together as a group.

This was so on one occasion when we were praying for a crusade which was to take place in another town, and we had prayed solidly in tongues for almost two hours. There was a point during that time when we knew we had broken through a barrier, for where it had been hard to speak in tongues and to make ourselves continue, there was a point reached when we could pray easily. The words flowed from us as if we would never be able to stop. The language which had been hard to bring forth, and which seemed of little value, was now pouring from our lips in authority; there was such a strong sense of victory in our midst. We knew we were declaring the counsel and authority of God far beyond our minds and our reasoning, and only by the enlightenment the Lord gave to us could we have any comprehension of what was accomplished that evening.

I had a vision of a fishing boat letting down its nets into waters that were mined. I asked the Lord for the meaning of the vision, and He said, "Your praying has removed the detonators from the mines." In other words, we had taken the power away from the enemy concerning the crusade that was to take place.

Excitement rose within us, and we could pray with our understanding that there would be a harvest of souls and a growth amongst God's people as a result of that crusade.

We now realise that the Body of Christ has an important function to aid the ministers. For too long we have left them to do everything — not only to study and preach the Word but to break through all the powers of darkness that may be preventing people from even hearing the message that God is giving to them.

17

A View of our Objective

Many books have been written on the power of our words, and I believe that those who have been used to write them have, through their own experiences with the Lord, known revelation concerning the power of the tongue or the power of words.

The Lord has been gradually revealing to me the importance of my words, and how what I say affects me or affects other people. He has also shown that the more I work in oneness with the Holy Spirit, the more powerful and effective are the words that come from my mouth in prayer.

Our words carry authority when we have been in communion with the one who has all authority. We can be so one with the Lord that we can speak His word that it might come to pass. In the beginning God spoke, and what He declared came into being; what came into being is kept in position by His word.

There have been times in prayer when His word has been declared through my mouth in order for something to come to pass. One evening, while seeking God and praying in tongues, I was reminded of riots that had taken place in Liverpool about ten days earlier. For a moment or two I could not imagine why the Lord had drawn my attention to something that had already happened, but as I continued to pray I found myself thinking of Ipswich — my home town — and I began to feel indignant and concerned. Surely riots were not planned to take place in Ipswich?

I stopped praying in tongues and said, "Lord, there shall be no riots in this city! Without understanding why I should suddenly make that decree, I knew an authority as I spoke those words. I did not ask God to protect Ipswich; I made a declaration that came forth from my mouth by the power of the Holy Spirit.

The next day, Saturday, I went to the centre of the town in the early afternoon and found to my amazement crowds of young people standing around. It was new to see the centre of our town occupied in this way, and there was an atmosphere that I had not felt before. I noticed a shopkeeper coming out into the roadway and looking apprehensively at the crowds, and I thought "They have come to town," for I knew that they were not all Ipswich young people. As I walked through the midst of them, I said, "Lord, this has already been dealt with."

Two days later I received information via a young policeman, who said that the police had had the tip-off that there was to be a convergence on Ipswich. They had been on the alert and had made preparations for trouble, but I was given to understand that they were surprised at the way the young people had dispersed and left the town without any commotion. God had spoken in the situation! The Holy Spirit had found someone on their knees through whom He could channel the message, in order that the creative words to stop a riot could go forth.

I had often wondered why I called Ipswich a city when I was in prayer, for I was well aware that this term was incorrect and that Ipswich is a town, but it felt good to call it a city.

After I had been away for two nights I had a real sense of excitement at the thought of returning to Ipswich. I felt I could not return quickly enough and never before had I experienced such a feeling.

On the brow of a hill I was able to cast my eyes over the town where I had lived since I was six years old. With much joy and delight I thought, "My Ipswich; I love my Ipswich." It was just as if I loved the streets and the buildings, but I told myself that it was ridiculous; we are supposed to love people, rather than buildings and streets.

Days went by, and I still pondered why I should suddenly love Ipswich and call it a city when it had no cathedral. I decided to look at the dictionary definition of the word 'cathedral', not realising that the Lord would give me enlightenment on what I had been feeling and experiencing.

I read these words — "Cathedral: contains the bishop's throne, the seat of authority." I then knew without a doubt what the Lord was saying to me — that there is a seat of authority, not in a building made with hands but in the heavenlies. I remembered the Scripture that we are seated together with Christ in heavenly places (Ephesians 2:6), and realised that it was from that position that we should operate spiritually — dealing with principalities and powers of darkness which rule over towns and cities and influence men and women in an evil way.

Just as the Children of Israel were given the Promised Land and were told to go in and drive out the enemies who were reigning there, I believe that we too have to take the spiritual authority which is ours in Christ Jesus and drive out the enemy who has been reigning in our place. **"The weapons of our warfare are nor carnal, but mighty through God to the pulling down of strongholds" (2 Cor. 10:4).**

When we take our rightful position and go against the powers of darkness under the direction of the Holy Spirit, we shall speak the words that need to be decreed. We shall loose that which has to be loosed and bind that which has to be bound. This position will not just come out of a knowledge of the Scriptures; it will come out of a walk and oneness with the author of the Scriptures.

An influx of Moonies came to Ipswich, and this cult was sucking many young people into its ranks. Many Christians were disturbed about their activities in the town, and I was asked to join petitions that were being raised to have them removed.

I felt that whilst petitions and complaints are important, my part — and the part of the fellowship to which I am joined — was to seek God in prayer concerning this situation. It was while we were praying in the Spirit that the Lord gave me a vision.

I saw one of the old-fashioned brown earthenware sinks that were seen in kitchens of bygone days. These were unglazed and preceded the white glazed type which can still be found in use. I could not imagine why the Lord was showing me that old brown sink, until I asked Him what He had to say to me through it.

He took my mind back to when I was a child, and had visited two aunts with my mother. I could hear the conversation which took place between my mother and those aunts. My mother had said to them, "Why don't you have a modern white sink put into your kitchen?" and they had replied that they had asked the landlord to replace the sink but he was unwilling to do so.

My mother had immediately told them that the brown sinks had been condemned by the Health Authorities, and that if anyone in a rented property did not wish to have a brown sink they could demand that it be changed. If the landlord refused to do this they could call in the Health Authorities who would enforce the removal and replacement of those sinks.

My faith came into operation immediately! I knew what to pray under the guidance of the Holy Spirit. I called upon the Higher Authority to come and deal with that which was condemned, and I declared that the Moonies were to be removed from our town.

Nothing happened for quite a while. The Moonies were still around for a time, but the word of God had been decreed and He knows how to bring His word to pass.

Imagine my surprise when many months later one of our national newspapers won a case against the Moonies condemning them nationally.

I am well aware that there were undoubtedly other people praying concerning the matter, but I also dare to believe that even if no-one else had prayed, God had been able to declare His word and His mind in the matter and His word is final.

Does this mean that I can now influence every area of the town's activities? Does this mean I am praying about everything concerning the local government and the administration of Ipswich? No, it does not, for of myself I can do nothing. I too can only speak the words that I hear, and I too can only do that which I am led and instructed to do by the Holy Spirit.

I believe that as I go on to know the Lord and to seek His face, I shall know more and more about what to loose and what to bind in His name. I believe that each member of the Body of Christ can be so led in prayer that our presence upon this earth will be felt and known — not by what we preach but by the effects of our communion with God.

The Lord gave me another experience to show me the power we have within us and the power expressed through our words. I had a husband and wife staying in my home and, while hurriedly working in the kitchen, I accidentally burned the three middle fingers on my right hand. I rushed to the tap to apply cold water to the burns, and tried not to be affected by them as we sat at lunch. I wrapped a clean handkerchief round my fingers, trying to block out the air in the hope of decreasing the pain.

The husband turned to the wife and said, "Pray for Freda that the pain be taken from her." The wife took hold of my hand and asked the Lord to remove the pain and to heal the fingers.

Immediately the pain left. I removed the handkerchief and looked at the inflamed swollen areas, particularly the middle finger which had been burnt more than the other two. I gave thanks to the Lord for the immediate miracle wrought by His power.

My guests left soon after lunch, and later in the afternoon my younger daughter came to see me. I started to tell her what had happened — how I had burned my fingers and how I had had prayer and the pain was gone.

As I talked to her I looked at my three fingers — still burning red, still uncovered and yet without pain, and I said, "There should be pain in those three fingers."

I was only in conversation with my daughter, telling her what was a natural fact, for without covering or medication on burns the pain would normally be felt for quite a time. Immediately those words came out of my mouth, pain returned to my fingers. I could hardly believe it! It was just as if I had freshly burnt them, and I held my three fingers again in protective action against the pain.

"Oh, Lord," I said, What have I done?" I realised that my negative words had produced a negative result; but I thought "I only stated that there should be pain in my fingers to emphasize the miracle that there was no pain."

I quickly said to the Lord, "Please, can I have the good of my friend's prayer again. I am sorry I cancelled out Your miracle. Will you please now take the pain away once more." To my amazement the pain left my fingers immediately.

I could hardly believe that my casual words could cancel out what God had done and that the words from my mouth were so powerful. I had never known anything like it before and I certainly determined that I was not going to speak in such a way concerning my fingers again.

The next day, before making a long journey in the car, I looked at my three fingers. The inflammation in two of them had subsided, but the middle finger was still very inflamed with a small flat white patch in the centre. As I looked at it I thought, "There shold be a blister on that finger." Within fifteen minutes I had the largest blister imaginable.

"Lord, I didn't say the words, I only thought them and they came to pass!" The pain did not return to my fingers, but it was a little uncomfortable holding a steering wheel with an enormous blister on my middle finger. I did not dare venture to speak to the blister but just let it be dealt with naturally over the following days.

I was astonished at what had taken place. Was the Lord now telling me that my thoughts are as powerful and creative as my words?

18

A Daring Venture

"S.O.S. for prayer," said a member of my fellowship on the telephone one day.

A young Christian living in the same town as this member — some twelve miles away from me — was expecting her first child and had suddenly developed severe pains which were not labour pains. She had been taken to hospital and was being given drugs to alleviate the pain, and the whole family were worried about her condition and about the unborn baby.

I did not know the young woman concerned, but my friend and I prayed together on the telephone. We prayed in English and I asked the Lord to heal the young woman and to protect the unborn baby in every way, even from the effects of the drugs that were being given to the mother.

The next day my friend telephoned to say that

there had been no change in the young woman's condition and it was thought that there would have to be a Caesarian section in order for the baby to be saved.

The following day I had another news bulletin stating that the doctors had diagnosed the mother as having some disease of her muscles and would not be operating. My friend went on to say that the family were even more worried and distressed about the situation.

I answered, "We must hold what we have taken in prayer from the Lord," to which she replied "Amen."

The next day the news bulletin had not improved, and my friend added that she felt we needed to do more praying. We agreed that we would both take the whole of the morning in our own homes to pray in tongues for the young woman.

I replaced the telephone receiver and was about to begin praying when there was a knock on my door. Visitors arrived and stayed the whole of the morning, and I was not free until twelve o'clock when my friend telephoned again.

"How have you been getting on in prayer?" she enquired.

"I have not been able to pray as I have had visitors," I answered. "Have you been able to get anywhere in prayer?"

"Oh, yes," she replied, "but I have been in such a battle. I have known battles before, but never one like this — but I know that I have broken through and everything is all right."

I then repeated a question I had asked on other days. "Don't you think you ought to come to the Ipswich hospital and visit the young woman and tell her that you have prayed?" I thought this was the most natural thing as she knew the person.

She replied, "No, while I was praying the Lord showed me that *you* were to go into the hospital and make the visit."

I agreed to do this if it was what the Lord had indicated, although only near relatives were allowed to visit. I wanted to talk to her when she was on her own, which would mean going outside visiting hours.

Almost immediately I went and bought a bunch of flowers and made my way to the hospital, telling the Lord that I wanted Him to open the door if it was His timing, but to keep it shut if it was not the right day or the best time.

I went to the reception desk about one-and-a-quarter hours before visiting time, and stated that I had flowers for a particular patient. Immediately I was instructed that no visiting was allowed as it was the resting time for all the patients.

I said, "I understand perfectly, but may I just take the flowers to the ward so that they can be given to the patient?"

They told me to go to the ward and to ring the bell, when someone would answer and take the flowers from me. I was over my first hurdle for I had got past the reception desk. I took the lift to the right floor and carried out the instructions I had been given. When the nurse opened the door, I told her I had brought the flowers for the young woman and asked if there was any chance of my being able to give them to her.

She replied in a concerned tone, "Oh, we have just settled her and are hoping that she will be able to get some sleep for she badly needs rest."

Immediately I said, "Oh, I do understand, and I would not want to disturb her. I will leave the flowers and perhaps I can come back some other time."

Just then another nurse appeared and asked "Who are these for?" On being told, she quickly added, "We cannot disturb *her.*"

Again in an apologetic tone, I said, "I fully understand and I will come back another time."

I was still holding out the flowers waiting for them to be taken, but the first nurse said, "Just a minute." She walked along the corridor, opened a door and peered into the room, and then turned and beckoned me.

I had been more than willing to retreat for I had no idea what I was going to say to that patient. I did not know her and would have been quite happy for God to shut the door, but obviously He was working in the situation and had gained my admittance.

"Hello, Sylvia," I said with a flourish as I entered the room, just as if I had known her all my life, since I did not want the nurse to discern that I was a complete stranger.

As soon as the door was closed behind me, I continued, "You do not know me but you know my friend, and we have been praying for you."

A boldness welled up within me and I continued, "Jesus has sent me." With my finger raised and pointed in her direction, in an authority which matched the boldness within me — I said, "You are going to have a normal delivery and your baby will be all right."

She whispered, "Just what I wanted to know. Just what I wanted to know."

I had no idea whether she was a new Christian or a mature one. I continued, "You need to rest in God's word. I know you need the natural rest, but you must also rest now in what He has said. Do you understand?" She nodded.

I asked her if she had prayed and again she nodded, "Yes."

"All right," I said, "I will not stay any longer, I will leave you to get some rest. The flowers were an excuse to get in, but they are with our love."

Upon that, I left the young woman. I did not pray with her. I did not have any further conversation with her. I had gone in and declared what was to be.

On arrival home, I was so amazed at what had happened. "Lord," I said, "I have entered that hospital and declared that she will have a normal delivery and that her baby will be all right, and I have spoken on the strength of what my friend said she had done in prayer this morning. Will you now give me a word?" The Lord said, "Read Psalm 107."

I turned to my Bible and read until I came to verse 20 — **"He sent his word, and healed them, and delivered them from their destructions."**

I said, "Thank You, Lord. You sent your word into the hospital and You have delivered this young woman from her destruction."

The next day my friend telephoned and said, "Freda, she has been able to move her legs."

I questioned, "What do you mean, she has been able to move her legs? Could she not move them before?"

The reply came, "No. Didn't I tell you?"

I must admit that I heaved a sigh of relief that I had not known that her condition was so bad when I went into the hospital.

The following day I received another news bulletin, stating that they had been able to get the young woman out of bed, and she had had a bath and her hair washed.

When the fellowship met the next evening I shared with the whole group that two of us had been in prayer for the young woman. I did not state what I had done, but I asked them if they would join in prayer for her.

We all prayed in tongues for quite a while. Afterwards I received word that she had started normal labour pains late that evening, and her baby was delivered normally during the early hours of the next morning.

Oh, the joy of working with the Lord! Oh, the joy of the power of His word flowing through us, and oh what joy for His people to work together in prayer. I realised that I had been able to trust the prayer life of another member of the Body of Christ, for I had gone into that hospital without checking with the Lord that He was sending me, but believing that my instruction had come from Him via my friend on the basis of the battle she had won in prayer.

19

Silence!

It took me many years to discover the value of silence in prayer. With my active nature and mind, it was an effort to wait long enough in a silence to discover if there was anything to be found in it. In other words I was too busy to meditate or I was too active to enjoy the presence of the Lord in a silent stillness.

For years I remained in a role that I can liken to a young person making friends with another and, yes, becoming intimate in love. I remained in that delightful stage of wanting to talk and share, like two young lovers who have so much to tell each other.

I grew and began to take on responsibilities in my walk with the Lord which I would compare with those of a young wife and mother, but it took me a long time to learn in my walk with the Lord what I had learned much more quickly in my natural marriage — the oneness and companionship, and enjoyment in silence of the one you love. To give love, adoration and communication without words is also prayer and a facet of our walk with the Lord.

There are times when I have known the love of the Lord as I have sat in silence with Him. This love has been reciprocated and expressed by the tears that have trickled down my face. I have sat in silence and have known what the Lord was requiring of me and what action He wanted me to take in a particular situation.

Oh that I had learnt this side of prayer much earlier, for it has a beauty all of its own and should play an essential and delightful part in the walk of every Christian. I had wondered if this could be experienced only by those who are older in years, naturally as well as spiritually, until I discovered through a planned silence what the Lord could do and how the younger folk could experience the Lord in this way too.

As a group, we decided to kneel in silence before the Lord for half an hour. This was something we had not deliberately done before, and we shared our experiences at the end of the period and discovered the value of time spent in this way.

A ten-year-old boy said he felt that the Holy Spirit was sponging us all over. What a lovely description the Lord gave to him — washed, or gently sponged, by the Holy Spirit. A nine-year-old who was present said that he had gained a new confidence for his work at school in the new term about to begin.

One lady in her late sixties said the Lord had reminded her of some things in her life that she had left undone, and other things that she had done which she ought not to have done. As He reminded her of these things, even though she had been a Christian for many years, she told the Lord she was sorry and knew His forgiveness. Before the silence had ended she had re-dedicated her life to the Lord.

We realised that many things had been achieved in that silence, but most of all there was a sense of contentment and oneness, not only between us and the Lord but between each other as a group.

In another planned silence at a prayer conference, I discovered how powerfully and freely the Holy Spirit can move. I also saw how we can interrupt the work of the Holy Spirit, and even stop or prevent what He wants to do.

During this silence one person reached out in faith to give a prophecy. It was obvious that this person had a heart of love and wanted to encourage all the others that were there with what the Lord had been giving to her as a personal encouragement. While there was nothing wrong in her wanting to give, the silence should not have been interrupted.

We are all having to learn and to discern that the Holy Spirit can move and work silently amongst a group of people without the use of the spoken word. A silence does not have to be filled. God's silences speak!

One woman shared with me afterwards that during the silence the Holy Spirit took her back to her childhood days and, I suppose like a psychologist, dealt with various issues that had put her into bondage. He took her through the events in her life that had prevented her from being a whole person and, as she responded to Him, He set her free. She emphasised to me that she *knew* she was free.

She explained that while she was in the midst of that personal interview and healing session with the Lord, it had been broken by the words that were given out in prophecy. Afterwards she tried to carry on but could not, and the Holy Spirit had to begin again and take her through the first stages. Then, in the continued silence, He was able to take her right through into freedom.

I believe she was led to share this with me because it opened my eyes to new depths of the working of the Holy Spirit and how with good intentions we can interrupt His lovely work.

Once we recognise that God by His Holy Spirit dwells within us, and that we do not have to find Him but only commune with Him who is within, we shall be awakened to the value and enjoyment of this silent communion.

20

Young Climbers

As a parent I became very conscious of God's word in Proverbs chapter 22 verse 6 — **"Train up a child in the way he should go: and when he is old, he will not depart from it."**

It took me many years to realise that training a child is not only telling the child what to do or what not to do, it is living the right life for the child to copy. The lives of parents, their actions, their methods, their outlook upon life, are the most vital part of a child's training.

Teaching a child to pray consists of far more than saying a grace before meals, or a rhymed verse with hands folded before going to sleep. Training a child to pray means he must be a part of the prayer life of the family.

For a child to value prayer, he must see how important it is to mother and father. Not only must he realise that his parents retreat to be alone with God — he must hear them praying and become naturally involved in the parents' communion with God as he is naturally involved with the other activities of the household.

Also, in the life of a church or fellowship, the children will develop and be affected by the growth in prayer of that community. I have observed with great interest and delight the way in which a child can not only become aware of God but can have a living and vital communion with Him.

The Lord found a way to reveal this fact to us as a fellowship. He had shown us that instead of having the children separately on a Sunday afternoon, we were to come together as a family — children and adults united to praise and worship the Lord and to be instructed together from His Word. This went against anything we had ever known, and against the training that some of us had received concerning Christian work amongst children.

One member of the fellowship, who had always been actively engaged in children's work, found this word from the Lord difficult to accept — not only because she preferred to work with children on their own, but because she could not understand how the children would get sufficient help and instruction on their level when in a meeting with adults.

She had no doubt that the Lord had told us to unite in this way because He had spoken separately to her about the matter, but because she could not work it out in her mind, she remained in a battle for a few weeks. In desperation she went back to the Lord and asked Him to help her to understand how the children and adults could be instructed together.

The Lord gave her a vision of the grown-ups and children sitting in a meeting, and said, "If you could take their bodies away, what would remain?"

"Their spirits would remain," she answered.

Then her eyes were opened to see what the Lord was saying to her. We are all spiritual beings; the difference that we see with our natural eyes is in the age and size of the bodies in which we live. When the Word of God is ministered by the power of the Holy Spirit, that word is spirit and life to all those that hear.

It has been wonderful to discover the way children are able to respond to the Word of God without necessarily understanding it with their minds. I have also been amazed to see how they can sit enthralled when the power of the Holy Spirit is upon the speaker, and the message is far above their natural intelligence and understanding.

One Sunday afternoon a four-year-old asked for a certain chorus to be sung. We started singing with half our attention upon the Lord and half upon the child who had made the request, but as we continued we became aware that the child was knowing a touch from God. I have never seen a four-year-old praise the Lord as on that occasion;

his eyes were alight as he sang and he clapped his hands in perfect rhythm. I believe that little child knew the power of God upon him. We sang and sang, repeating the chorus time and time again, until our hearts were meaning the words that came from our lips.

That same evening at bedtime he asked his mother, "Who is Jesus?"

She answered his question, only to receive the further request that he wanted to see Jesus. The mother explained as best she could that we cannot see Jesus with our natural eyes. The child was not satisifed and repeated, "But mummy, I ***want*** to see Jesus."

She had then taken him to the window and drawn his attention to the movement of the trees, pointing out that he could not see the wind but only the effect of the wind. So it is with Jesus, she explained; we do not see Him, and yet, as surely as we know the presence of the wind, we know the presence and the work of the Lord.

This still did not satisfy him, for he insisted that he wanted to see Jesus. She said, "All right, shall we tell Jesus that you want to see Him?"

His answer of "Yes" was immediate, and so the mother prayed, simply telling Jesus that her son wanted to see Him, and would He find a way to reveal Himself to him.

The child was content and was tucked up in bed.

After a while he called to his mother who was downstairs, and said, "Mummy, I know Jesus now."

No-one can know what took place in that child's bedroom that evening, but I have since watched him grow spiritually as well as physically.

When as a group we were learning to listen to the voice of the Lord, we had sat in silence for a while and then shared whatever the Lord had said to us. The whole purpose on that occasion was to listen to the Lord's voice.

It was so delightful to hear what the children had to say. One boy, his eyes wide with excitement, said that he had heard the Lord say to him "I love you." A seven-year-old received the word that "as the flowers bloom, I bloom in you." Another boy said he had heard the voice of the Lord and it was soft and gentle, not loud and shouting. To a five-year-old He had said, "I am your rock, not sinking sand."

Helping the children to hear the voice of the Lord is a vital part of their growth in prayer.

Two children with their mother were stranded in the country when their car would not start. The mother, knowing nothing about the mechanics of a car, repeatedly turned the ignition key with no effect. The little girl started to cry but her younger brother turned to her and said, "Stop crying and start praying!"

The mother needed this word too, because she had become anxious about the situation, but then asked her young son to pray. He immediately asked the Lord to make the car work. The mother admitted that she turned the ignition key again with much doubt, but to her amazement the car started. Her husband later said that it must have been a miracle because without a replacement part the car should have been inoperable.

I listened with keen interest one Sunday afternoon as a member of our fellowship told the story of Shadrach, Meshach and Abednego and how they were thrown into the fiery furnace at the command of Nebuchadnezzar because they had not bowed to the golden image which he had made.

I was puzzled as to why only three children had arrived that day, and began to feel that the Lord had something special in mind. I silently prayed and said, "Lord, only You know what has happened to the other families, and the reasons for their absence this day, but I believe You must have a very real purpose in bringing out the story of those three young men when we only have three boys present. What do you want us to see, Lord?"

He said, "I want you to pray for these three children."

After the word had been expounded, I shared what the Lord had said to me and we felt it important to gather round and lay our hands on the children. We waited for the guidance of the Holy Spirit as to what to pray and what to request on their behalf.

I then found myself praying aloud, asking the Lord to work upon those three in such a way that they would be bold like Shadrach, Meshach and Abednego; that they would be protected in any situation that could be likened to fire and that they would know the power of the Holy Spirit upon their lives, teaching them and leading them into all truth. I cannot remember all the words of my prayer, but felt I was praying for their protection more than anything, no doubt due to the story that had been given to us.

The next day the mother heard the four-year-old — the youngest of the three — speaking in tongues when he was playing. She brushed it aside, thinking that perhaps he was copying others he had heard praying in tongues. The following day she took the family to the swimming pool and, as that little one stood on the side of the pool, full of excitement and anticipation for the fun he was about to have, he began to speak in tongues again. She realised then that he had been filled with the Holy Spirit and had been given the gift of tongues. This had been solely the work of God, for we had not prayed deliberately for this and he had not received any instruction concerning the gift of tongues. The Holy Spirit had done His own lovely work in that child.

I know that many children are trained to give a tenth of their pocket money to the Lord, but I am also aware that there are those children who pray and ask the Lord where they are to give their money and how much they are to give.

On one occasion we had a special offering for a certain member of the Body of Christ. One mother told me how the two young members of the family retreated to their bedrooms to pray. They returned with the exact amount of money that Jesus had told them to give.

I have known the sick to be healed through the prayers of the children, and I believe that encouragement should be given continually to the young members who will one day be men and women of God, influencing the world and bringing glory to our Lord Jesus Christ.

21

Beckoning Heights

Just as love and trust are so interwoven and form an integral part of our knowing the Lord and responding to Him, so also are prayer and worship. To consider prayer without worship, or worship without prayer, is like trying to live with blood in our veins consisting of only red corpuscles or white corpuscles. One without the other is not possible, and an imbalance is not normal.

Worshipping God and giving to Him must be more important than anything else. Too often I have been so concerned about people's needs and my own problems that I have neglected to spend time praising and worshipping the Lord.

I believe that a life of obedience to God and a heart which is determined to fully trust Him in spite of hardships and difficulties is a life of worship to God. I feel we should also take steps to express our worship by singing His praises, by speaking words of adoration and worship, by silent communion with Him or even by falling upon our knees before Him — worship that comes from our hearts and from our lives being fully committed to Him.

I can so easily get caught up with my own little world and my family, or perhaps even the work He has given me to do, that I forget that I need to bless God and to exalt Him.

Just as there are stages of growth in every aspect of the natural life, so, I believe, there are stages of growth in the spiritual life. If we know new depths in prayer, where we experience a closer fellowship with the Lord, it follows then that we must enter new depths in worship. This will automatically mean transformation in our lives, changes wrought by the Holy Spirit to conform us to the image of God — for how can we enter new depths of prayer and worship without being changed more and more into His likeness. To worship Him in truth and in the spirit must mean that there is an inexplicable bond between the worshipper and the One worshipped, between the saved and the Saviour, between the sheep and the Shepherd and the seeker and the Found.

We are not the only seekers, for God Himself is a seeker. Jesus said that God is seeking those who will worship Him in spirit and in truth. (John 4:24).

One of my first experiences of discovering a new depth of worship took place in my own home while with a company of twelve and thirteen-year-old girls and just three or four adults.

We had been studying the life of Moses and had reached the part of the story where the Children of Israel had crossed the Red Sea in safety. We were reading the verses in Exodus chapter fifteen, giving the words that they sang to God, when one of the girls asked, "How did they know what to sing?"

I replied, "They must have been so thrilled with God that as they began to sing praises to Him the Holy Spirit gave them the words."

She then asked, "Can we do that?

"Of course we can," I replied.

They had been so enthusiastic to enter into a similar depth of praise as those Children of Israel that I found myself in a situation which I knew I could not handle. Their request was beyond my experience, and I knew that unless the Holy Spirit led us into that kind of praise we could not do it of ourselves.

I explained to them that we would all have to start using our voices to sing in English, believing that the words that came to our minds were the words given by the Lord, and that we would have to sing any tune and believe that the Holy Spirit would put us into harmony. In other words, we would have to begin in order to allow the Holy Spirit to take us into the experience.

They all agreed that they would begin, so I then prayed and asked the Holy Spirit to give us the words and to take us into a new depth of praise.

The result was thrilling! We began singing whatever words and tunes came to our minds, which at first sounded like a confused babble. But as we continued in faith, we became lost in praises to God and the harmony and the words were beyond our asking, and certainly beyond our natural capabilities. We came into perfect timing and harmony, and sensed the presence of God in a new way. We were of one accord and one heart, worshipping God under the leadership of the Holy Spirit.

On another occasion when I was with a group of approximately one hundred women, we began to sing in tongues and continued for a time. While I was conscious that I was having to take the initiative to sing in this way, I was aware not only of the presence of the Lord but of being led into being an integral part of the whole assembly in worship.

After a time the singing gradually died down and a brief silence followed. Then from the back of the group one lady began to sing words in English as given by the Holy Spirit and we realised that the tune was being given by the Holy Spirit too. The words poured forth from her mouth and the music of her song rose higher and took us into a depth of worship I had not known before.

I found something rising up within me that made me begin to express myself in almost a whispered song. This happened simultaneously with the rest of the congregation, and an observer would have thought that a conductor had given us the signal when to quietly and softly begin to give a background to the solo. They would then have thought that the conductor was causing us to bring in a harmony and a depth of accompaniment that only an experienced orchestra or choir could do. Our voices rose in united worship and a melody began to come forth which none of us had heard or learnt, with the soloist taking the lead. The pianist must have known the anointing power of the Holy Spirit upon her, for the soloist, pianist and assembly of singers were directed by the Holy Spirit to worship God in a choral performance that had not been rehearsed.

Part of my endeavour and my faltering steps to worship God has been not only by praying but singing on my own, and I have found that in singing God's praises I want to repeat the words time and time again; for not only do I mean them, but I discover that I enter into new depths of fellowship with the Lord and new depths of commitment.

The words pour out from my lips repetitively, for my heart is not satisfied with saying "I love You." It desires to go on saying "I love You" and "Oh, how I love You" and "I do love You, Lord."

Whatever the expression or the content of the words may be, sometimes the repeating of them takes me into a depth that is not found in an instant or the once sung verse or hymn.

A small group of us began to sing a well-known hymn, the words bringing tears to some eyes, and various verses were repeated as individuals felt free to lead the repetition. Other choruses and verses of hymns were sung and without our planned intention, without our requesting, the Holy Spirit took us into another new experience of worship. In between the well-known hymns and choruses we found ourselves singing in tongues. The Holy Spirit then helped us to express our own words of adoration and thanksgiving and worship in English — sometimes using a known tune but other times with tunes that came to us as fresh as the words we found to sing. Not only were we free to sing in adoration and worship, we were free to lift up our hands to God, to stand or to kneel.

I realise that I would not have found that place of worship without the others in the group, and that we all needed each other for the two-and-a-half hours which were spent in simply worshipping our wonderful God.

My desire to worship God has gradually become stronger, and I believe I can liken the desire to that of a mountain climber. The more time a climber spends climbing, the more he desires to climb. The more a person worships, the more he will desire to worship, and while I have reached a few summits, I am constantly aware that there are other mountain peaks to be climbed. There are heights that seem to be out of reach, and yet stand with a beckoning challenge to the desire within my heart, making me take fresh steps to continue.

22

Persistence

There are two stories in the Old Testament which I believe stand as monuments giving examples of how to walk in complete trust in God and how to press through difficult circumstances in faith.

Joseph, the favourite son of Jacob, was hated and ill-treated by his brothers. They threw him down a pit and then sold him to a company of Midianites who were going to Egypt. I can well imagine those merchants selling Joseph when they arrived in Egypt; I can easily imagine a market scene and Joseph even being auctioned as a slave, and I have often wondered what he thought as he stood there miles from home and the father who loved him, a foreigner stripped of his rights and privileges, standing amongst a crowd whose language he did not understand.

Potiphar, an officer of Pharaoh and captain of

the guard bought Joseph, and we see that the Lord was with Joseph and he prospered in the house of his master, for he found favour in the sight of Potiphar as he served him faithfully. Potiphar made him overseer over his house and all that he had was put into Joseph's hands. We read that God blessed the Egyptian's house for Joseph's sake.

After a time the wife of Potiphar dealt treacherously with Joseph, and, because he refused to succumb to her enticement, she lied and presented a story to her husband which meant another downfall for Joseph. Potiphar took him and put him into prison.

Through all of these circumstances there is no record that Joseph ever complained; there is no record that he became downhearted or frustrated, or rebelled against God. In fact the story shows the opposite, for the Lord was with Joseph and gave him favour, not only in the sight of Potiphar but in the sight of the keeper of the prison.

My imagination does not give me a wonderful picture of prison life in those days, and no doubt our prisons of today are palaces in comparison. However, Joseph's trust in God must have been complete.

We read how he interpreted the dreams of Pharaoh's chief butler and baker when they were thrown into prison and how, when they were released, Joseph asked them to remember him and make mention of him before Pharaoh — stating that he was stolen out of the land of the Hebrews and had done nothing wrong that he should be put into the dungeon. They forgot him, and Joseph continued in prison — still without complaining — for another two full years until Pharaoh had a dream and the chief butler remembered that there was a man in prison who could interpret dreams.

Many times when my situation could have overwhelmed me and I have been near to hanging my head down in despair and discouragement, the Lord has said just one word to me — Joseph! I knew what He meant and would immediately raise my head and lift my heart to God, determined that Joseph's testimony would be my encouragement. I would tell the Lord that I wanted to be like Joseph — trustworthy and willing to stand in the midst of trials and difficulties and hardships. I wanted to please God by trusting Him.

There was nothing that Joseph could do to change his circumstances, although I believe we could say that he did change them because of his trust in God; but he had to go through the hardship in order for God to fulfil His purposes and bring him to the prominent position of ruler over all the land of Egypt.

We may not be called to an important position in the church or in the world, but I believe we are called to follow Joseph's example of trusting God.

My encouragement in faith and prayer comes from the story of the woman in 2 Kings chapter 4. When she saw Elisha she would invite him into her home to eat, and later she suggested to her husband that they build a separate room where he could stay.

We read how Elisha wanted to do something for the woman, and when he learned that she had no child he called her and said, "**About this season, according to the time of life, thou shalt embrace a son.**"

Her reply was, "**Nay, my lord, thou man of God, do not lie unto thine handmaid.**"

I had often wondered about her reply. What did she mean? I could not believe that she was doubting the word of Elisha, but for a long time I could not understand her answer. Only after reading this story many many times, and meditating on her actions and her words, could I perceive the depth of meaning in her statement to Elisha, for in other words she was saying, "I expect your word to come to pass, because I will not receive a lie from you. I receive your word and the fulfilment of it."

What faith, and what a challenge! It is the way we should receive God's word.

The story continues of how the woman conceived and brought forth a son, and when the child was grown he was out with his father in the harvest field and became ill, and the father instructed the servant to carry the child to his mother. She sat him on her knees until noon and then the child died.

The mother then went and laid the child upon Elisha's bed. She shut the door and went out and called her husband, asking him to send one of the young men and an ass so that she could go to the man of God.

Her husband enquired why she should go to Elisha, seeing it was not a special day, for he said, **"It is neither new moon nor sabbath."**

She answered him, **"It shall be well."**

I am amazed at this point of the story. She did not fling herself into her husband's arms, as most of us would have done, sobbing and lamenting that their only child, their son, had died. She did not even tell her husband what had happened for it was obvious that she was not going to accept the death of her son. Her words **"It shall be well"** were a part of her journey of victory.

She took the first part of that journey when she laid her son upon the bed of Elisha. We must remember that communication with God in those days was through the prophets and the men of God. By placing her boy on Elisha's bed, she was in effect putting the matter into God's hands, expecting Him to act on her behalf.

She then saddled an ass and said to her servant, **"Drive, and go forward; slack not thy riding for me, except I bid thee."**

As she approached Mount Carmel, Elisha saw her afar off and told his servant Gehazi to run and meet her and to enquire whether it was well with her and with her husband and the child.

Gehazi obeyed, and my heart leaps for joy as I read her answer to Gehazi, for she said, **"It is well."** How many would have said "It is well," knowing that their only son was lying dead at home? Not one negative word came from that woman's lips, not even to the servant of the man of God.

She came to Elisha and caught him by the feet, and Elisha knew that her soul was vexed within her and that God had kept the matter hidden from him.

She asked, **"Did I desire a son of my lord? did I not say, Do not deceive me?"**

She was determined not to have communion with anyone except the man of God, and to remind him that she expected his word to stand. She was not giving up the child which had been given to her by the Word of God, even though he had died.

Elisha gave instructions to Gehazi to take his staff and go immediately and place it on the face of the child. This did not satisfy the woman either, for she said, **"As the Lord liveth, and as thy soul liveth, I will not leave *thee*."** She was only going to have the highest in the situation, for we read that Elisha then arose and followed her, and when he saw the child dead upon his bed he went in and shut the door and prayed unto the Lord. The child came back to life and was presented to his mother.

No faithless words had come from the mouth of the woman. She had only communed with the man of God, and was determined that his word to her remained in complete fulfillment.

There must come persistence in our praying, and a laying hold of God, where we will not accept defeat or what our circumstances dictate to us. If we will rise up like that woman and commune only with God, presenting Him with His word and the promises made under His covenant, we shall not utter faithless words for **"whatsoever is not of faith is sin." (Rom. 14:23).** We will not accept the circumstances but only the word of God as the answer. We will make our journey in prayer to the end result; no matter how devastating the circumstances may be, we will make that journey of faith, with singleness of heart and mind, letting only the word of God dictate in the circumstances.

We must have the determination to get through in faith, which Jesus spoke of in the parable given in Luke chapter 11. A man went to his friend at midnight asking for the loan of three loaves of bread. The friend answered, **"Trouble me not; the door is now shut, and my children are with me in bed; I cannot rise and give thee."**

Jesus said that because of his importunity, the friend did rise and give the man bread. He then followed this story with the words, **"Ask, and it shall be given you; seek, and ye shall find; knock, and it shall be opened unto you. For everyone that asketh receiveth; and he that seeketh findeth; and to him that knocketh it shall be opened."**

From these stories we see that persistence in

prayer, coupled with consistent faith, brings life into the situation. The Lord said in Matthew chapter 7 verses 13 and 14, **"Enter ye in at the strait gate: for wide is the gate, and broad is the way, that leadeth to destruction, and many there be which go in thereat: Because strait is the gate, and narrow is the way, which leadeth unto life, and few there be that find it."**

I had always thought that those two verses applied to the sinners and the saints; the sinners were on the broad way that leads to destruction; and the saints had found the narrow way which leads to life.

When I was in prayer one day on behalf of another member of the Body of Christ, the Lord gave me those words, and it took me a while to understand what He was saying. The broad way is the way of the sense realm. If the great woman in 2 Kings chapter 4 had accepted the sickness and the death of her son, which was opposite to God's word to her, she would have been on the broad way. Because she believed the word given to her by the man of God, she had to press through that strait gate which was narrow and confined and restricted.

This strait gate can be any position of difficulty perplexity or distress; in other words, the tragedies and the challenges in our situations are like a gate preventing us from entering on to the path of life.

The woman not only made the effort to get to the man of God; her speech was in line with what she was determined to have. She only declared, **"It is**

well." The sickness and death which made up her strait gate did not prevent her from getting on to the narrow path which led to life.

A battle of faith and a persistence in prayer is needed to get through our own difficulties and perplexities. In spite of many defeats in the church we must still apply the word of the Lord in persistence and get through the strait gate in our situations. We must be determined to get bread in the middle of the night of our difficulties. This walk of faith has to be taken step by step and it is important that we learn how to overcome even concerning smaller details and less vital issues of life.

I remember that I was deeply grieved and hurt over what was said to me by a dear friend. She had looked at my situation, weighed up the details and felt that I was taking the wrong action, that I was not seeking the Lord and that I was doing my own thing. Her torrent of words hurt far more than any pain I had previously experienced, and I went home wounded and distressed.

In the confines of my own room I poured out my heart in tears to the Lord, because I knew that only He could help me. Her words rang in my ears and I felt that I would never be free again.

I wept and prayed until I knew I was released from the hurt and until there was no sting left in the words. I then went on to pray for my friend, knowing not only my love for her, but I believe I experienced some of the Lord's love for her too. I was amazed at the words that came from my mouth, for I said, "Lord, lay not this to her account, but to mine."

Joy welled up within me because the Holy Spirit had taken me to a place where even the blame for her misguided thinking, and some of the things which were uttered which were not true, would not be laid to her account but to mine. The love of the Lord through me set her free from any effects that could come upon her, as well as setting me free from the hurt and bitterness which could have resulted from that episode. I had pressed through all that could remain a blockage, or in other words I had gone through the strait gate and had found the narrow way which led to life in the situation. If I had not done that, or found that place with the Lord, I believe I would have been on the broad way which would have destroyed so much in me.

Hurt is a destroyer, bitterness is a destroyer, and the long reaching effects of such an episode can cloud one's thinking and one's confidence, yes, and even one's walk with the Lord.

I pressed through another strait gate after my younger daughter had gone to New Zealand on a prolonged visit. I missed her company and chatter and the fellowship we had known together. I knew that the Lord had opened the door for her and that it was right for her to be in New Zealand, but there was not only an emptiness in the home, there was an emptiness in my heart.

I felt as if I had a cloud over me and realised that I

had to get free from it and to find an answer from the Lord. I told Him about my heartache even though I was confident that He had arranged the circumstances and that it was His plan and purpose for her to be in New Zealand. I was honest and told Him how much I was missing her, but I knew it was not right that my days should be gloomy because of it and I asked Him to help me.

I prayed in tongues, determined to get through all that I was feeling. I love the way the Lord comes to our aid to direct us through the gate when He sees our persistence.

The Lord gave me a vision of a brick wall, and I saw my daughter walking towards the wall and then walking right through it, leaving a hole or gap which was exactly her shape. I said, "Yes, Lord, that is the gap that I feel."

I realised that no-one else could fill that gap; there would be no-one else in the world that would exactly fit that shape inch by inch, and no-one else was meant to fill it.

As I continued to pray in tongues I saw a cloud come and fill that hole in the wall. I knew then that the Lord Himself had filled it by the cloud of His presence, and I thanked Him. I had found that narrow way which led to life.

I stood upon my feet and rejoiced. I can honestly say that from that moment onwards I did not pine or feel at a loss because of the absence of my daughter.

23

Determination

Ten days before I was due to leave for the United States of America, I discovered on waking that I could not move without severe pain in my back.

I had gone to bed feeling perfectly normal and, as far as I was aware, I had not done anything that could have caused the pain. I could not sit upright in bed, and as I tried to move the pain made me gasp or groan.

Eventually I managed to get out of bed by rolling and lowering myself to the floor on my hands and knees, slowly getting upright on my feet; this took time and was very painful. My mind immediately wanted to know what was wrong. Had I pulled a muscle, or did I have a slipped disc?

I turned from my negative thinking and used various Scriptures in prayer. I thanked God that **"He is the Lord that healeth,"** and that when Jesus died on the cross **"He bore all my sicknesses and my infirmities, and by His stripes I was healed."** I thanked Him that I am meant to "prosper and be in health even as my soul prospers." I remembered that when Jesus walked upon the earth, none that went to Him for their healing were turned away without it.

So I prayed for my healing and received it by faith, but continued to walk in pain. I found that I could not take my normal length of step or bend from the waist, and I was unable to do my usual quota of daily work.

I had promised to visit some friends in Manchester prior to going to the United States of America, and I did not relish the journey in my car or the effort of staying in someone else's home, trying to appear normal and walk in health.

I thought that as I went I would be healed, but the journey was a trying one, and getting in and out of the car gave me excruciating pain.

I wanted to hide the fact that I was being challenged in that way, but almost immediately on arrival I was asked, "Is something wrong with your back, Freda?" I had a hot water bottle given to me to enjoy while sitting on a chair.

Climbing the two flights of stairs to my bedroom did not make life easy, and the effort of getting in or out of bed or even doing anything was so tiring and painful that I was not sorry when the weekend was over. As if going home would heal my back!

I was bowed down with the thought that I had a much longer and more arduous journey to make in a week's time, and began to wonder how I was going to cope with my back in that condition. A friend had previously volunteered to drive me to Heathrow Airport. Other friends in America had offered to meet me, and I began to believe that this was special help being given to me by God because of the state of my back.

I had discovered that if I made the effort of putting myself into a hot bath, I had ease from the pain for a little while. It felt good while I was in the bath and I thanked the Lord for healing me, but the pain continued.

One morning I decided that I had to take stock of the situation. I told the Lord that I did not have a problem believing what I read in the Scriptures; I did not analyse it, and even if it seemingly did not work for me, that did not change His Word. I knew that I could not change it to fit my situation; my situation should change because of His Word. So I concluded that the Word of God was no problem to me, because I believed that when He died on the cross it was a full salvation for my spirit, soul and body.

It began to dawn on me that my body was not the problem either. It was under attack, but the real problem was in my mind for I did not think in healing or in health. I was only thinking in the painful condition — even to arriving in America in pain, being unable to lift my cases, so that the Lord had arranged for me to be taken care of by being met.

Suddenly I knew I had found the key! My mind needed to be renewed — my thinking had to change. Instead of catering for the wrong condition, I had to think in the right condition — to think in health.

I slowly put myself into another hot bath and as the hot water soothed my weary body, I determined to change my thinking — even about the tasks waiting to be done before I flew to America.

I spoke aloud, and said, "Lord, I just do not know how my back will be able to keep in its wrong condition when I do all that I am going to do today!" Normally I would have said, "I just do not know how I am going to do all the work that needs to be done, with my back in this condition."

As soon as I heard the words which I had spoken aloud to the Lord, my faith was stimulated further. Without stopping to think I got out of that bath, not considering pain or catering for it, and began to jump up and down. Then I said, "Lord, the first thing that I am going to do is to bend over and clean the bath."

This I did immediately, without letting another thought come to my mind. I bent my body for the first time for days and I was free from pain.

I then declared that I was going to do another cleaning job which was waiting to be done and which would need much bending and back work, I rejoiced and worked throughout that day, cleaning the house and packing my case. I had found the key! My thinking had changed and so had the condition in my back.

That evening, a young woman from the fellowship arrived and asked, "How is your back, Freda?"

"Under authority!" I answered.

It was wonderful to be free from pain and I climbed into bed that night without any effort, rejoicing in Jesus and thanking Him for healing me.

In the morning, not realising what I was doing, I thought, "Shall I leap out of bed, or shall I get out carefully." I began to move carefully and discovered my back to be full of pain yet once again.

My heart sank. Where was yesterday's victory? Why had I lost it so quickly? The Lord had healed me — what had gone wrong? I decided to ignore the pain in my back, concluding that it was a lie. Ignoring it did not make the pain go away and I spent another day in misery. I went to bed early, thoroughly fed up with myself and my condition.

I remembered that there was one thing I had not done according to Scripture, for it says **"You shall lay hands on the sick and they shall recover."** So I pushed my hand under my back and said aloud, "Lord, You said that 'you shall lay hands on the sick and they shall recover' and I am putting my hand on my back and I am commanding it to come into line with Your Word."

Immediately my back clicked and I was then not sure whether it had been put right or whether something had gone out of place! I found myself lying in bed with a multitude of negative thoughts about my back. I could not sleep that night because I was worried and my flight to the United States was all too near.

I rolled out of bed the next morning and discovered that my back was far worse than it had been previously. I said, "Oh, Lord, I am in a muddle and I got out of bed the wrong way, for I got out in my condition — I did not get out of bed in You."

My determination began to come back into action and I continued, "Lord, I am going to put myself back into bed, and I am not getting out until I get out in You and in Your Word."

Stupid as it may seem to be, I painfully put myself back into bed in order to get up the right way — that is with my thoughts upon Jesus and not upon my wrong condition. Having accomplished the feat of getting myself horizontal again, I then asked the Lord, "Do You have anything to say to me, Lord?"

He replied, "Be of good cheer, I have overcome."

I answered, "Right, Lord, I will get out of bed on

that word."

My downcast feelings were abating and I again placed myself in a hot bath. I then asked the Lord what I should do next. He told me to pray for a lady I knew, who had been crippled for eighteen years. I almost groaned on her behalf, for I could begin to empathize with her in her pain and in her thinking; realising how hard it must be for someone who has been afflicted for any length of time to find the key to release their faith in the provision of God.

I spent a time praying in tongues for her. After a while, and before the bath water was cold, the Lord gave me a vision of Himself holding a whip. I could not see Jesus very clearly, but the whip was clear and it looked horrible. I could see metal or glass pieces at the ends of the leather thongs, and I said, "Lord, why are You showing me a whip?"

He answered, "This is the tool that gave me my stripes."

As He spoke, He presented that whip to me. Although I could have recoiled from the horrible implement, I stretched out my hand and received it as a flag-bearer having been presented with battalion colours. My mind then went to the spectacular occasion when our Queen presents the colours or flag to a battalion, and how she stands back and takes the salute while the colours are marched past and the men of the regiment follow.

I knew that I had been presented with the greatest banner and in my mind's eye I could see

Jesus standing back to take the salute as I marched past in honour of Him and all that the whip represented. I realised that many others would also follow behind me in the same regiment and my heart was overwhelmed with joy. My mind was at peace and I quietly got out of the bath completely free of pain. The pain never returned.

I had pressed through the strait gate and found the narrow path that led to life in my body.

I was taken to the airport and met, not because of a physical need but purely because the Lord delighted to give this added pleasure to my journey.

24

Pressing Through

I am so used to walking carnally — according to my five senses — that I can very easily drift along the broad way, for it takes effort and determination to not only seek the Lord for His word but to walk in it.

The wide path has a wide gate, which is influenced by what I see, hear and touch and by what I feel and say. Anyone's opinion and word can take me along that broad way and I am kept there by my own reasoning and lack of effort to break from old habits.

I can be so accustomed to the broad way that when I am faced with challenges I can react in the same way as the man or woman who does not know God.

When sickness comes, we can take the word of the doctor as the only word for the condition and his instructions as the only word for the cure, which may or may not work. We can have other opinions, which may or may not help.

The broad way is far easier because we travel it with our senses, and we are so used to living in the sense realm. It is less effort to go with the tide than to go against it or to find another way to that which is the usual way.

The narrow path which leads to life is different because we can only have one person's word to get onto that narrow way. We can only have one person's opinion, one person's instruction — in fact, only one person is the Way.

In 2 Corinthians chapter 5 verse 7, we read, **"for we walk by faith, not by sight."** Wuest's translation says, "for through faith we are ordering our manner of life, not by something seen." I believe the faith we have been given is big enough to move a mountain, but to get past our knowledge and feelings concerning our challenges we need help from the Holy Spirit so that our faith can come into action.

Asking, seeking, knocking, represent degrees of increasing importunity and supplication. I do not think this necessarily relates to our spiritual growth, but depends upon the situation and how active our faith can be without the hindrance of our reasoning.

There are times when I can ask the Lord for something and know that I can receive it by faith.

Other times I have to seek Him, perhaps because I do not know what to ask, or perhaps because my mind with all its knowledge and information about the situation prevents my faith from asking.

Knocking, I believe, can be likened to the story of the woman in 2 Kings chapter 4, for she was determined to have life in her situation.

The woman in Mark 5, who had been ill for twelve years, and had spent her money trying to get help from doctors, determined in her heart that if she could just touch the hem of Jesus' garment, she would be healed. The strait gate for her was not only that she had been ill for twelve years and the fact that the doctors could not help; she had to go against the Jewish law and her reasoning of what would happen if she touched anyone. She did not accept the situation; she determined to have what she was after and made her own choice of pressing through her strait gate and receiving life.

The Syrophenician woman who went to Jesus to get help for her daughter had to press through the fact that the disciples wanted to send her away, and the words of the Lord when He said, **"I am not sent but unto the lost sheep of the house of Israel."** All of those details together with her daughter's calamity constituted her strait gate.

If she had taken them all at face value, or with her reasoning, she would not have found the narrow path that gave life in her situation. As we look at this story more closely we discover that the details which could defeat us are the avenues through which our faith can move. The Lord's words to that woman were so phrased that she could give an answer which would not only keep her faith active but enable her to reach out for the ultimate.

When we seek the Lord, He finds a way to speak to us that will stimulate our faith and keep it active until we have the answer or the goal for which we are reaching. His words to us when we seek Him help us to press through our strait gate, because He wants us to press through.
her faith complete, for He said, **"O woman, great is thy faith: be it unto thee even as thou wilt."**

When we seek the Lord He finds a way to speak to us that will stimulate our faith and keep it active until we have the answer or the goal for which we are reaching. His words to us when we seek Him help us to press through our strait gate, because He wants us to press through.

We *must* take note of what He is saying to us, giving it careful thought, for His words are the vehicle which carry us along in faith to touch Him or to receive what we are needing.

My friend telephoned me one day and said, "Another S.O.S. for prayer, Freda."

I silently sighed, and thought, "Not another one!"

She went on to explain that a person she knew had been telling her about a baby in the north of

England who had been rushed into hospital in a serious condition with meningitis.

This person had asked my friend if she knew why God allowed such things to happen to babies. My friend had answered that while she did not understand everything, she did believe in prayer, and said that she would pray for the baby and the family. The telephone call was to request me to pray also.

I agreed and hung up the telephone, and thought to myself, "If I do not pray now I shall forget."

I did not find it easy to pray for an unknown baby of an unknown family somewhere in the north of England, and, as far as my friend knew, this family did not know the Lord.

I knelt down and began to pray in tongues, with little or no active faith. There are so many sick babies all over the world, how could I reach out in faith for just one of them?

To help myself, I began to imagine how I would feel if this were my baby or my grandchild. I suppose that was my first effort to press through the strait gate. I then began to weep, and secretly thought that I would have to weep my way through in intercession. Immediately the Lord said to me, "Why are you crying?"

I stopped and said, "You mean, Lord, I do not have to cry?"

Through this question and my answer, my faith was alerted and went into action. Without hesitating, I asked the Lord to heal that baby and to bring it into complete wholeness so that there would be no after-effects from the meningitis. I also asked the Lord to find a way to move in that family so that they would know that God had healed the child and also know that He loved them.

By the time I had finished praying, not only did I see the baby healed but I had asked the Lord to save the family too. His word to me, "Why are you crying?" was the avenue through which I could move in faith; in fact that simple question made my faith complete. I could ask and receive, my reasoning and knowledge no longer a barrier to the path of life for the baby.

I received news about a week later that the baby had so responded to treatment in the hospital that the doctors had said they could not give any reason why there should not be a one hundred per cent recovery.

I believe that as we go on in the Lord, not only will we press through the strait gate and find the narrow way of life for ourselves, but we shall find it on behalf of others.

I was rather concerned to learn that my brother had developed diabetes and had begun to have trouble with his kidneys or bladder. This additional trouble was creating a real problem for him.

After many days I began to get similar symptoms

in my own body. I prayed and thanked the Lord for healing me, but the discomfort continued and I thought I must have developed the same complaint as my brother.

During that time I travelled to the other side of the country and was perturbed not only by the symptoms but by the inconvenience of the problem. I did pray for my brother as well as for myself but I had no idea what was happening.

On my return home the condition in my body did not improve — in fact it began to get worse, and one particular evening I knew increased discomfort which was distressing.

The next morning I met my brother's wife, who was very concerned. "Something must be done," she said, "for all his nights are disturbed and last night the problem was far worse."

I thought, "This is no coincidence. Yesterday evening was the worst time for me." Had the Lord permitted me to feel in my body some of the things that were wrong in my brother's body?

As I thought about it, I realised that my nights had been completely free. Not one night had been affected but his nights were always disturbed. If I really had the same sickness, I would be troubled at night too. Only during the day did I experience the symptoms.

Why had I been so slow to realise what was happening? I then went into prayer on behalf of my brother, no longer trying to get healing for myself but just interceding on his behalf. This went on for a few days, until one evening the Lord said to me, "It is complete."

Every symptom left my body and I was free. I knew that my brother was free also. I went to see him the next day and shared how the Lord had laid his trouble upon me, how He had caused me to enter into prayer on his behalf, and that I knew the matter had been dealt with. He had already begun to have ease, and during the following week the problem disappeared.

25

A Bid for the Summit

In 1969 my husband Percy had a serious illness and was not expected to live. The severe stroke, as a result of a massive clot of blood damaging the brain, presented me with a challenge and a dilemma such as I had never known before. I desired with all my heart to face the challenge in the Lord, and I asked Him for a word for my situation.

I told the Lord that I would accept whatever he gave to me, whether it was life or death. He spoke to me and gave me a clear word from the Scripture that my husband would live and would be raised up. I believed this word and held it firmly in spite of every evidence that was contrary to it.

The doctors had told me that there was nothing that could be done for Percy. He went to the lowest depths of unconsciousness, from which patients do not recover, his eyes were open and fixed, and in the natural the situation was hopeless, but I believed God and the word that He had given to me.

When he did not die, I was told that he would have to be moved to a long-term nursing hospital. I asked for him to be returned home where I knew that I could not only nurse him but minister life to him.

I saw remarkable changes and witnessed many exciting details. During the first eighteen months at home he began to walk and do things which the doctor declared were beyond medical knowledge.

The next eighteen months he was looked after in various hospitals, simply because I had laid down the word that God had given to me and the Lord had directed me to ask for him to be taken care of outside the home. No medical treatment could be given to him; he was just fed and looked after. One arm and hand remained paralysed for several years; in fact as this arm and hand hung lifeless at his side, it began to have an adverse effect upon his shoulder. His fingers were completely set fast and lifeless. While in hospital they put the paralysed arm into a sling in an attempt to support the shoulder, and a splint to aid the drooping wrist, in order to give him a little more comfort.

The Lord in His own wonderful way showed me that He wanted me to take and hold again His word of life for Percy, and after the lapse of eighteen months he returned home to me, when I imagined that the healing would flow much faster than ever before. I attempted to put the paralysed arm into the sling on his return home but he refused to let me do this.

Very gradually the use came back into that arm and hand. My son-in-law had taken the battery out of our car to get it recharged, and hurriedly placed it in an outside shed on his way to work, stating that he would call on his way home to refit it. Later that day I went outside to look for Percy, and discovered the battery was missing from the shed. He had carried it to the garage which was at the bottom of our garden; he had opened the garden gate and the garage doors and had lifted the battery into place in the car and connected it correctly. For a hand and arm that should never have come back into operation it was a miracle.

I know the power of God's word, for there was continual progress during the eight years that my husband lived. Though he remained incontinent and never did speak again, he travelled with me wherever the Lord sent me. I took him to many areas of Spain, also to Denmark, Sweden and Finland, because I not only stood on the word that God gave to me but I endeavoured to obey and follow his instructions.

It was while I was in Sweden that the Lord opened my eyes to the ministry of the Body of Christ. The depth of love that flowed through the Swedish Christians enlarged my horizon and my vision as to what God can do when He has freedom to move through us. They took us into their homes and loved us. We stayed for two weeks with one family and I saw more healing come to Percy's body, for he responded to God's love ministered to him — the love that is so powerful, the love that can do anything. My heart soared at what I discovered and the way the Lord gave to Percy through the Body of Christ.

My situation and my story did not work out how I thought it would originally, for the healing was not completely manifested in all parts of Percy's body, and I can only liken my walk concerning the word for his healing to an attempt at climbing the highest mountain.

I had the privilege of staying in the home of a man who was a member of Chris Bonington's team that attempted to climb Everest in 1972 by the hardest route at the most difficult time of the year. As he shared with me the hardships they had to face, the difficulties that had to be overcome and the singleness of purpose needed as a team, I saw a little more about my own trek of 'mountain climbing.'

Although on a major climb only one or two people normally reach the summit, they could not get there without the whole expedition being planned and carried out by each member of the team. I began to see what the Lord was showing me, for I believe He is preparing a body — the Bride of Christ — who will so work together in unity that a climb of victory will not only be attempted but will be achieved, so that the banner of the Lord will be set up on high and His name glorified.

My friend described how, when they were ready to tackle a most difficult part of their climb near to the top of Everest, high winds had blown all the snow off the Rock Band that had to be climbed and which barred their route to the summit. The Rock Band was unclimbable without the snow, and although sufficient supplies to meet their needs were available, although there was enough stamina left in the climbers the freak winds had prevented them from reaching the summit.

There can be many reasons why I did not reach the summit concerning the word that I held for Percy. I understand that a mountaineer must have an abundant supply of determination that will last him through to the top, for on the ascent the determination gradually decreases. The hardships of the climb diminish the strength too, and unless there is complete teamwork the whole expedition is doomed to failure.

Seemingly there was a 'Rock Band' without snow near the top of my 'mountain' so that I could not reach the summit. The full reason for this, I do not know. I cannot say that my faith remained in the same strength as when I started the climb, or that my determination did not ebb. I cannot say that the words of my mouth and my confession remained perfect like the woman in 2 Kings chapter 4. I cannot say that my seeking God concerning my situation was constant; and I believe the fellowship to which I bclong would agree that their experience as 'climbers' did not make a perfect team for climbing.

I believe that in the last days it will not be just a few individuals achieving some outstanding walk of faith, but I believe it will be a united walk of faith by those climbing as a team. It will not be one person glorifying the Lord, it will be the Body of Christ glorifying Him — working in unity and oneness, under the guidance of the Holy Spirit.

We need to do our own individual climbing in our own personal situations, in order that we might become strong members of this wonderful expedition. We need to develop our own personal prayer lives in order to be effective members of a praying body. We must all as individuals be determined to get through to the Lord, yet knowing that our determination makes us a part of a united team.

The stamina of a climber can only be produced as one climbs. Behind any outstanding performance of skill lies not only hours of work but commitment and a forsaking of other pursuits. We must lay hold of our goal to glorify the Lord Jesus, developing our fellowship with Him and pursuing Him like Elisha pursued Elijah — making a choice to find our position, like John resting his head on the breast of Jesus, where he could ask intimate questions.

Committing ourselves to this goal and being determined to achieve it, we shall have fulness of joy and the evidence manifested of our oneness with the Lord.

This pathway of achievement has to be walked step by step, with renewed daily determination and dedication. The speed at which we walk or climb is governed by us and not by the Lord. It is influenced by how much we seek Him and how much we desire His will, and by our obedience and response to what He shows us.

Two years after Percy went to be with the Lord, the importance of teamwork or being united in prayer was again brought home to me as I sought the Lord over a number of weeks. I believe the Holy Spirit directed me in my praying, for I found myself burdened concerning the many afflictions that are to be found upon God's people — some who have been crippled or sick for years, as well as those who have mentally handicapped children. I found myself daily naming those that I knew, crying out to God on their behalf.

I told the Lord that I realised that His gift of healing had been coming more and more into operation in the Body, because I knew that many had received direct healing from Him; He had raised up ministries through which a number had been released from their bondages and afflictions, but I pointed out to the Lord that there remained so many unreached afflicted people.

Every day I found myself praying in that way, until on one occasion I expressed myself in picture language, stating that these afflicted ones seem to be locked up in a city on their own, surrounded by a high wall which we could not penetrate. I reminded the Lord of what had happened at Jericho and how He had given instructions to Joshua and the Children of Israel; I said that I knew that even while they obeyed His instructions, it was His power that brought down the walls of Jericho.

I then said, "Unless You give us instructions, this high wall will remain and the afflicted members of the Body of Christ will not be able to get out to us, neither can we get to them."

After praying that day, the burden lifted and I no longer found myself calling upon God in the same way.

About a year later I was in Sweden and one young man shared a vision that the Lord had given to him and which he did not understand. He had seen a high wall and in it was a very large gate; many people were pushing on that gate, which was on wheels. When eventually it was opened, he said that wild plants began to come out through the gateway.

I asked the Lord to give me the vision so that I could see it clearly too. The Lord revealed to me that He was answering my cries to Him that had taken place months previously. He had used the same picture language that I had used and had shown me that in the high wall round that city there was a gate. In my mind's eye I could see that the gate had been shut for a long time; in fact it seemed to be rusted in place and not one individual could open it.

Team work and a united effort will be required to push on that gate to get it open. Once opened, the 'wild plants'—or afflicted people of God—will be released to come out from their imprisonment and from that 'city of affliction." I believe that as the people of God pray and intercede concerning some of the chronic conditions, God, by His power, will open the gate of their release as effectively as He brought down the walls of Jericho.

Ministries have been placed in the Church by God until we come to unity of faith. In this unity we shall push on that gate — we shall climb the highest summit — we shall decree what has to be decreed — we shall know how to be led in prayer and shall have authority over the works of the enemy.

At the wedding feast in Cana the best wine was saved until the last. While staying in a Christian home in the United States, I enjoyed being able to help myself to the grapes that were growing in the garden. I returned to that home for a brief stay in the autumn and my host commented that there was still a bunch of grapes on the vine, which surprised him because there had been night frosts which normally killed any remaining grapes.

After my last meal there we felt it would be good to have communion, but my host declared that he had no wine. I suggested that we squeeze the juice from the grapes to use for our communion wine. This we did, and when it came to the point of sipping that 'wine' I was so amazed at the taste. I watched my host as he tasted the juice of the frosted grapes and we knew that not only was it special for that occasion, but that the Lord was saying something to us through that event.

Many months later I was staying with a family in Germany, when the husband began to talk about wine. He stated that there was a very special one which he had never felt free to buy because it was so expensive. I enquired what made that particular wine so special and expensive, and he replied "It must be made from grapes that have had the frost."

The best wine is being reserved until the last. We may feel the frost as we climb and we may know situations that are cold and bleak — but just as men have climbed Everest and have been determined to go on in spite of the hazards and bleakness, we too must go on seeking the Lord — not to achieve success for ourselves or by ourselves, but to be part of a team who will raise up a banner upon this earth that will glorify our wonderful Lord Jesus Christ — a team that will be poured out like wine which the Lord can taste and enjoy — wine made from grapes that have remained through any frost which could have destroyed them.